Simple Boat Electrics

Simple Boat Electrics

John Myatt

Copyright © Fernhurst Books 1997

First published 1997 by Fernhurst Books,
Duke's Path, High Street, Arundel,
West Sussex, BN18 9AJ, UK
Tel: 01903 882277 Fax: 01903 882715
Printed and bound in Great Britain

The moral right of John Myatt to be identified
as the author of this work has been asserted
in accordance with ss. 77 and 78 of the
Copyright, Designs and Patents Act 1988.

British Library Cataloguing in Publication
Data:
A catalogue record for this book is available
from the British Library.
ISBN 1 898660 25 5

Acknowledgements:
The author and the publisher would like to
thank George Durrant and Ewan Aburrow of
Ampair of Poole for their assistance.

Cover design by Tim Davison
The photograph of the Trintella 51 on page 10
is by Christel Clear.
Cover photograph and some photographs of
diesel engines by Chris Davies

Photographs of the renewable energy
sources by Ampair, Poole

Photographs of the sequences on soldering
and multimeters are by Ewan Aburrow

All other photographs are by Julia Claxton
and John Myatt

Design and DTP by Creative Byte of Poole

Edited by John Carden

Printed by Hillman Printers, Frome

While every effort has been made
to ensure that the advice given in this
book is correct, the publishers cannot
accept any liability for the outcome
of any particular recommended
course of action.

Write, phone or fax the publisher
for a free, full-colour brochure.

Contents

Introduction

Flick a switch: a light lights up – turn a tap and water runs out – to cook a meal simply press a button or turn a tap and on comes the heat.

At home this is so normal you hardly think about it since all these resources continue in unlimited quantity so long as you pay the bills. If something goes wrong within the system you pick up the telephone and someone comes to sort it out.

Your home is part of a complex network supplied from the centre. A boat is more like an island, or a remote community. There is no continuous supply link with the outside world. It is an independent system with finite resources. Those resources must be replaced, or reproduced, by you, as they are used. To do this, raw materials have to be made, found, or imported and various sub-systems have to be maintained. The inhabitants, the crew, must be able to keep all these processes going. The most vital resource to the system is electricity.

It is perhaps surprising to realise that this is a fairly recent luxury. A hundred years back most homes did not have it. On a yacht, even fifty years ago electricity was unheard of except on the very largest luxury vessels. Now we take it for granted. Taking things for granted usually leads to trouble.

The raw material for producing electricity on a boat is normally petrochemical fuel – usually diesel, though other sources are available. The mechanism for producing electricity is a generator, driven off the engine. The generator converts mechanical into electrical energy. Since you don't always want to run the engine when you need electricity, you must store some of it for use later. Batteries are used for this purpose. A

Using a starting handle in a limited space is not always possible. Better to keep the battery topped up.

battery does not strictly store electricity, as we shall see, but it is the next best thing.

One battery must always have some reserve because it's required to start the engine. The high compression ratio in a modern diesel engine makes it difficult to start by hand cranking, and the installation sometimes makes this impracticable anyway. Muscle power alone won't do!

There are four basic needs for an electrical system: a generator for producing the electricity, batteries for storing it, a network of wires to distribute it, and an electric motor to crank the engine and get the whole thing going.

You can of course treat these systems, and all the circuits or equipment items they supply, as 'black boxes'. 'Black Box' is a term often used in science to describe a system in terms of inputs and outputs only. The trouble

with this approach is that when things inside the box go wrong you are in trouble unless you can replace the whole box. A detailed understanding of how it all works is not essential but some knowledge of what is happening can save a lot of tears. It can help you to repair some faults and so save money, and make you safer at sea.

This book opens the boxes. It tells you how they work, explains their use and care, and explores any limitations they may have. The aim is to take a practical but low-tech approach to keeping it all going properly. Theory is limited only to what is necessary for understanding.

ELECTRICITY AND SALT WATER

A boat at sea is about the worst possible environment in which to use electricity. All sorts of nasty things happen when salt water and electricity meet. Some of these things are obvious as soon as they happen. Others tend to creep up on you without much warning – unless you can anticipate them you may easily get caught out. I hope this book helps you keep your electrics in good order and keeps the juice flowing on your boat.

1 First principles

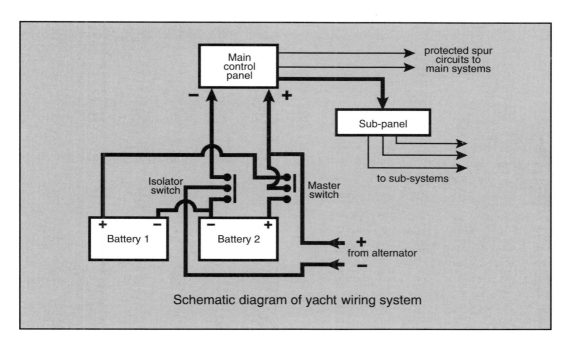

Schematic diagram of yacht wiring system

When a boatbuilder chooses the power source and storage components for a new electrical system he starts at the end and works back towards the beginning. He decides first how much electric power will be needed to run everything on the boat. Hopefully he will also allow some extra capacity for the additions that most owners make. Only then will he plan the system to meet these needs. Power is what matters: all electrical devices use power.

THE RELATIONSHIP BETWEEN VOLTAGE, CURRENT, RESISTANCE AND POWER

Power is the ability to do work and work is the conversion of one form of energy to another.

Electrical power is measured in watts (after James Watt of steam engine fame).

A generator creates a potential difference between its output terminals. Until it is applied to the ends of a conductor and starts to do work it is only a potential, because it produces no energy changes. The potential difference gives rise to a pressure called the Electromotive Force (EMF) which is measured in volts. Voltage is thus the force that causes a current to flow in the conductor, allowing work to be done. How fast the actual current flows depends on two things: the size of the EMF and the resistance of the conductor.

Imagine an electricity supply as being like a domestic water system. The potential difference (in this case hydromotive force) equates to the mains pressure where the

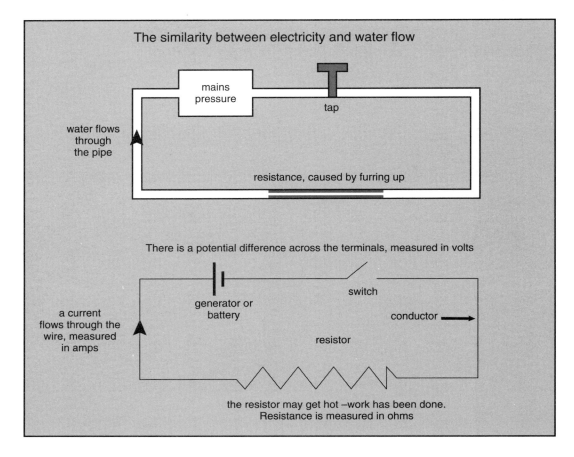

The similarity between electricity and water flow

water enters your home. The current is the flow of water and the conductor is the pipes in your plumbing.

The resistance is represented by the length, boundaries and nature of the pipes. A long thin pipe will result in a slower current since this means more resistance. Any obstruction in the pipe, maybe some furring or a poor coupling joint, will also affect the resistance and thus the flow rate of the current. A tap behaves much like an electrical switch.

Both electrical and water conductors have boundaries. A hole in a pipe is similar to a break in the insulation covering an electrical conductor. The insulation equates with the walls of the pipe. Any break in these boundaries will not stop the flow – indeed it may cause a greatly increased flow with catastrophic results in both cases.

Ohm's Law

There is a simple mathematical relationship between EMF, current and resistance. The relationship is defined by Ohm's Law. This states that the current in a conductor is proportional to the applied EMF and inversely proportional to the total resistance. EMF (E) is measured in volts, current (I) in amperes and resistance (R) in ohms so, put more simply:

$$E\ (volts) = I\ (amps)\ x\ R\ (ohms)$$

Power available

Suppose the water power was supplied in a channel or canal and was being used to

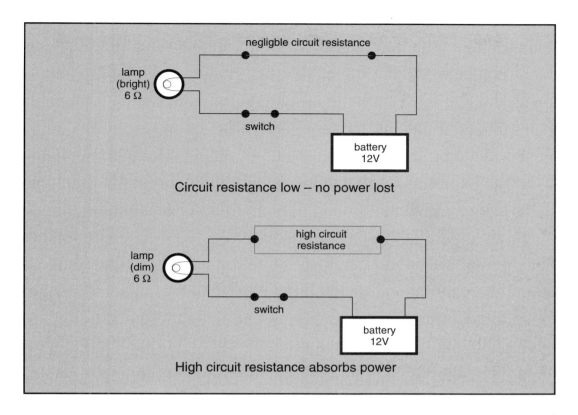

negligble circuit resistance

lamp
(bright)
6 Ω

switch

battery
12V

Circuit resistance low – no power lost

high circuit
resistance

lamp
(dim)
6 Ω

switch

battery
12V

High circuit resistance absorbs power

grind corn in a water mill. Clearly the work it could do would depend on the three things discussed so far: the force, the current and the resistance to flow. Ideally, we want no resistance in the stream because resistance will mean energy being wasted to overcome it. We will always prefer as much water as we can use to be available at the mill. Sadly life is not like that, and there is always some resistance (and loss of power) in the stream or, in a circuit, in the wires.

Power & Ohm's Law

Power is concerned with the rate of doing work. The rate is found by multiplying the EMF by the current. This gives another mathematical relationship:

P (watts) = E (volts) x I (amps)

So we finish with two simple equations. Since only one thing is different in each of them, the two equations can be combined to enable us to express any one component as a function of any two others.

Hence:

$$I = E/R \quad R = E/I \quad E = P/I \quad and \quad P = I^2 \times R$$

Try the following simple example to see how this works: A 12 volt supply feeds a light having a resistance (R_1) of 6 ohms. From $I = E/R_1$ we get a current of 2 amps. The power (from $P = I^2 \times R_1$) would then be 2^2 6 = 2 x 2 x 6 = 24 watts. The same result would come from the equation E x I = P (12 x 2 = 24 watts).

The resistance of the conductor wire in this example was too small to consider. R_1 was the resistance of the light only. A poor conductor (with a bad connection perhaps) producing an extra 1 ohm resistance in the circuit would increase the total resistance (R_t) to 7 ohms. The EMF is fixed so this voltage must be shared between the lamp and the wiring, so

Very high voltages are used to transmit electric power over large distances, because the power loss is much reduced.

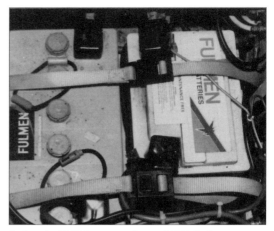

In boats 12 V (or sometimes 24 V) is the highest voltage used, for reasons of safety and weight reduction.

the lamp gets only six sevenths of 12 volts, which equals 10.3 volts. The current through it would be 12/7 = 1.7 amps.

The power dissipated at the lamp is thus $I^2 \times R_1$ or $1.7^2 \times 6 = 17.34$ watts (72% of the original value); with 2.89 watts ($1.7^2 \times 1$) being lost in the wire. The apparently missing 3.77 watts is the reduction in total power due to the decreased current.

The actual light output will be reduced still more, to less than 60% in fact, since much of the power is used to heat the filament. Full light only comes when the filament reaches full heat.

The important thing to note from these two equations is that a small increase in conductor resistance will cause a large reduction in lamp efficiency. This is the key to many of the electrical problems in boats.

The effect of increased voltage

Small changes in circuit resistance become less important as the supply voltage is increased. This is because less current is needed to produce the same power. If you do not understand this try some sample figures in the equations above. How much current would be needed by a 24 watt device with a supply voltage of 240 V? How much power would be lost by this current flowing through wires with a resistance of 1 ohm? Conductor losses are much reduced when the current is low. That is why electricity supply companies use very high voltages to move electric power over large distances.

The obvious question is: Why don't we use higher voltages in boats? There are two main reasons. One is that high voltages can kill. Our body resistance is fixed. It is actually the current that kills you but a higher voltage will mean a higher current. In practice any voltage above about 50 V can produce enough current to kill some people. The risks of shock in a humid, salty environment are high. Safety is thus one limiting factor.

The other reason is to do with the micro-world that is our boat. The only way a battery can give higher voltages is by being bigger. Bigger means heavier and the existing mass of a boat's batteries is already a problem. Some larger boats in Europe use a 24 V system (which almost doubles battery weight for the same power output) but very few use any higher voltages. In the USA, 12 V systems are standard and are the most common in the UK.

CONDUCTORS

Clearly the conductor joining the appliance to the supply is an important part of the system. The lower its resistance the less power is wasted.

Conducting wires are normally made from copper, which works well. (Silver is the best conductor but the best is too expensive. Silver is confined to such things as switch or relay contacts where low contact resistance is important.) By making copper conductors thick enough, and the length of runs short, the losses in them can be kept within sensible limits.

Copper does not corrode very quickly, even in salt water, but does suffer from electrolytic action. Water getting in between the conductor and its insulation can be a major problem. Marine grade wire has its strands coated with tin to reduce the damage but this is more expensive than plain copper and is seldom used on leisure craft. Some special grade wires have a resin filler added, which virtually eliminates water penetration.

A problem with copper is its softness. It means that small terminals cannot be made of the same metal as the wire. Screw connectors are often either brass, which reacts very little with copper, or plated steel, which reacts a lot. Use of mild steel connectors leads to serious electrolysis problems and should be avoided.

Any conductor heats up when a current flows in it. Provided the correct size of wire is used, this should cause no problem but most insulation is softened by heat so it is wise to use a heat-resistant grade insulation in hot areas such as engine compartments. Some marine grades of wire have two layers of insulation which gives better protection.

INSULATORS

An insulator is a material which stops the flow of a current. Many substances are used for insulation. Things like junction boxes and switch bodies must be rigid or semi-rigid while wires need highly flexible protection. Materials to be used as insulators on boats must be unaffected by water, salt, oil or fuel. They must be able to do their job in hot, damp, vibrating and gyrating conditions. They must also be able to do it for long periods without attention in the hidden depths of a boat's structure.

PVC (polyvinyl chloride) is used for all wiring where the ambient temperature will not exceed 65° C. In high-temperature locations, such as for heaters or cookers, EPR (ethylene propylene rubber) is more common.

Most marine-grade wiring has two layers of insulation to do the job but single-sheathed automotive wire is often used for additions. There is a difference between sheathing and insulation which is not often appreciated.

Insulation is primarily for electrical protection and may not be very strong physically. Sheathing has the primary function of providing mechanical protection. Sheathing will be used to prevent chafe damage to the individual cables in an extension lead, for example. Many modern materials provide both mechanical and electrical protection and this is where the confusion arises.

Twin-cored cables have insulation round each wire and sheathing combined round the outside of the pair for greater protection. The inside single wires should not be stripped from their cable and used without their sheathing.

ELECTROLYSIS

When two different metals are connected by a conducting liquid, called an electrolyte, they develop a Potential Difference between them. This is the principle on which a battery works, as we shall see in Chapter 3. Such a situation often exists accidentally in the damp, salty environment of a boat. When this happens one of the conductors, called the anode, breaks down physically as the current flows. If this is happening in your electrical system, you've got problems! The solution is to choose the metals carefully so that the PD is small, and to avoid their getting damp. It may sometimes be necessary to replace inappropriate metals, even in a new boat. The key to which metals to use can be found in the Galvanic Table. Metals that will come in contact must be close together in the Table if electrolysis is to be avoided.

Galvanic Table

(showing common metals found on boats)

Anode +
Magnesium
Zinc
Cadmium
Pure Aluminium
Light Alloy
Mild Steel
Cast Iron
Soft Iron
Active Stainless Steel *
Lead
Manganese Bronze
Brass
Copper
Silicon Bronze
Pot Metal
Nickel
Monel
Passive Stainless Steel *
Cathode —

*Note: The position of stainless steel in the table depends on its grade.

2 Generators

A generator converts mechanical energy into electrical energy through magnetism. It consists of a number of coils of wire which are wound onto an iron core called an armature. This is caused to rotate within a magnetic field (often provided by other, fixed coils). Rotation of the armature is supplied, via a drive belt, from the engine.

OUTPUT

Broadly speaking, the power available depends on three things: how fast the armature rotates, how many wire turns there are in the coils, and how strong the magnetism is. The first of these is dependent on the engine speed and the second on construction. The third is the factor that can be controlled during use. Clearly if the power output was to be fixed, the voltage developed is going to increase as the resistance of the external circuit increases, thus reducing the current. Similarly, the current would become excessive at very low load resistance.

In theory, as the generator is rotated faster the power available could continue to increase until it destroys itself. In practice, however, the maximum power produced is limited by design to avoid such damage. The components that do this form the regulator circuit – the details of which need not concern us. The regulator, by controlling the strength of the magnetic field, ensures that the actual output current available is substantially flat above a certain speed. The EMF to be developed is pre-set and depends on the voltage needed by the external circuit to be supplied. Nevertheless, open- or short-circuits should be avoided since either makes great demands on the circuitry.

Generators can be made to produce either AC or DC (alternating or direct current) outputs. The nature of the basic generating method means that all the electricity produced fluctuates between a maximum value and zero. It can also change direction. Thus strictly speaking all generators produce alternating current. Generators with a DC output are called dynamos. In a dynamo the directional changes are reversed by an electro-mechanical process whereas AC generators, called alternators, do not do this.

REGULATORS

All modern generators are alternators producing a repeatedly reversing output. This output is converted to a constant direction by a diode circuit within the alternator. This provides direct current for use in the boat, at the output terminals. So called 'Smart' regulators can adjust the output voltage by sensing the state of the batteries. In doing this they are able to avoid overcharging which, if unchecked, reduces battery life.

Alternators are lighter and more efficient than the old-fashioned DC dynamos and the output is taken from the fixed field coils rather than the rotating ones, making them more reliable. They can also handle much greater currents size-for-size. The components that regulate the output are frequently built into the unit to avoid damage to the system.

When the engine is running, the alternator output supplies all the power demands of the boat's electrical system; it also charges the batteries. If demand is too great, the alternator won't cope and the batteries won't

This battery control switch can be set to off, battery 1, battery 2, or batteries 1 and 2.

This ignition switch is located in the cockpit. To switch the engine on, turn the key. To stop it pull the lever, wait for the light or buzzer, then turn off the key.

charge properly. There must always be some load on the generator. Without it all the power produced would be dissipated internally as heat and would quickly destroy the alternator. This is why the battery switch should never be set to 'off' when the engine is running. Although these switches are of the type called 'make-before-break' it is best not even to change batteries once the engine is running. Nor, in many older systems, should the ignition switch be turned off while the engine is turning since this may also remove the load. Some more recent engine circuits are designed so that the engine is stopped using the key. In such cases either a dummy load is applied while the engine is stopping, or the output field circuit is broken by the switch so that the magnetic field collapses instantly. The manufacturer's handbook will tell you whether this applies to your engine.

COMMON FAULTS AND SYMPTOMS

Servicing an alternator is generally beyond the capabilities of the boat owner. However, you can check whether an observed fault lies within the alternator or not. Modern alternators usually contain three output windings and so need several diodes to turn the AC into DC – if one fails it may reduce the output rather than stop it.

Low or no output

Lack of output, or in some cases low output, will cause the charging or ignition warning light on the engine control panel to glow or flicker when the engine is running at normal speed. This may be accompanied by an audible whistle (alarm sound).

The whistle alarm is often wired as a common indicator linked to several possible engine faults. If it sounds, you will need to find out which one is the cause of the problem. Start by checking any other indicators fitted. If the charging light is out when the alarm sounds, you should suspect either a lack of oil pressure or overheating. Stop the engine at once. Allow the engine to cool and check the oil and coolant levels.

If the charging light stays on at high speed, stop the engine and check the drive belt.

1

Fan belt tension should be ±12 mm (1/2 in). Belt slippage can result in slow water pump and alternator speeds, but over-tightening will reduce bearing life. To adjust, first loosen the mounting bolts.

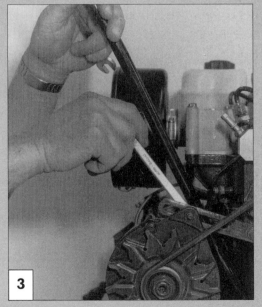

2

This bolt on a sliding stop regulates the alternator position relative to the belt, and hence the tension. Two spanners may be needed if a locknut is fitted.

3

Tension the belt against the alternator using a bar as a lever. Then tension the adjuster bolts. Finally, tension the mounting bolts.

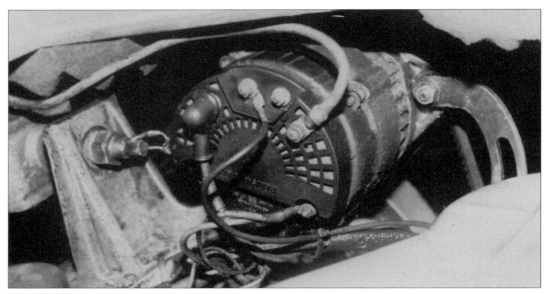

Check for breaks in the alternator wires, and for tightness in the terminals.

Should the warning occur only at low engine speeds, it's likely to be the regulator that is at fault. Try increasing the engine speed until the light goes out and then returning to idling speed. If the light now stays out you haven't a problem. When the light stays on at high speeds the alternator may not be turning, so check the drive belt.

Broken or slipping belt

A broken belt will prevent the alternator turning and must be replaced. A slipping belt will allow the alternator to run slowly or to stop and if this happens the belt may soon wear through and break. Belt tension is important. It can be adjusted by slackening the mounting bolts holding the alternator and moving it as shown on p.19. There should be about 1–2 cm movement in the middle of the longest section (depending on its length) under finger pressure. Over-tightening can cause undue wear to the alternator bearings. A more accurate adjustment, though less easily meas-ured, is a deflection of 4–5% of the total span.

Electrical connections

If there is still no output with the belt in order and the mountings tight, check for continuity in the exciter earth return wire (the thinner of the three wires connected to the alternator). A break in it will prevent any output. A high resistance joint in this wire can act as a voltage limiter preventing the alternator from prod-ucing its full output. Boat alternators are rarely earthed via the engine body except on some older road vehicle engines which have been customised for marine conditions. If no exciter wire is fitted, the earth return will be via the case. Next check the tightness of the terminals at both ends of the thick connecting wires.

Where a battery voltmeter is fitted to the control panel (sometimes one is included in the wind/log instrument control box), check the reading with the engine running and with it stopped. There should be a noticeable difference between the two readings if the alternator is outputting current. A multimeter put across the charging battery's terminals will do the same job.

Checking the tightness of all connections

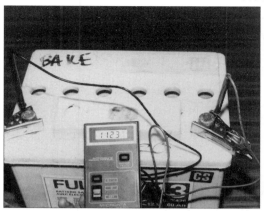

Using a voltmeter across the battery terminals with the engine (a) running and (b) off. A good difference in reading shows the alternator is working.

A two-pulley system: the water pump is driven directly.

is an obvious but often overlooked procedure. The ohm range on your multi-meter, or a continuity tester *(see Chapter 9)*, can be used to check for internal breaks in the wires. Disconnect the batteries before using an ohmmeter. If you find a break in continuity, change the whole wire.

GET-YOU-HOME TREATMENT

If you haven't solved the problem after all these checks, you are going to have to manage without a cure. Before replacing a broken belt check that the alternator doesn't feel over-hot and that it turns freely by hand. If so it will generally be safe to run the engine even without alternator output.

If the belt was the problem, and you haven't a spare belt available, check the number of pulleys it should run on. Where there are only two pulleys, the water pump will be directly driven by the engine and you can run it safely without a belt. Three or more pulleys and you will have to replace the belt before starting up. A single lay removed from a length of 12 mm (or thicker) nylon rope, woven into a loop, will provide a temporary belt if you have no spare. The length of rope

you'll need will be approximately three times the length of the broken belt.

A diesel engine doesn't need electricity to make it run. Without a belt fitted, there won't be any alternator output so the batteries won't be charged. Running without a belt, or with a makeshift belt, are short term, get-you-home measures only. On such a trip you'll need to conserve all the battery power you can. Switch off as much of the lighting and as many of the instruments as possible.

SERVICING

Where a fault is isolated to the alternator it is best to turn to the experts. Full testing requires special equipment and the replacement of faulty components is a task for the professional.

It is a useful precaution to remove the alternator during the winter overhaul and have it checked out. Before doing so, carefully label each connection and its associated wires to make refitting simpler.

3 Storing electricity (or battery basics)

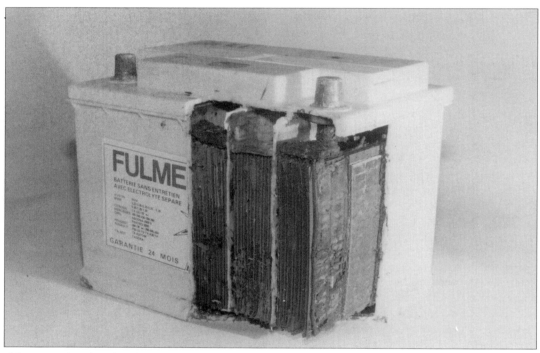

A battery, showing the plates.

Most people will tell you that a battery, or cell, stores electricity. Strictly speaking this is not true, but for most practical purposes we can safely pretend that it is. Electricity can only be stored very briefly without changing it to some other form of energy.

What a 'storage battery' actually does is convert electrical energy into chemical energy. When the battery is 'used', that chemical energy is converted back into electricity. You need to know this only because, in the course of conversion, some of the energy is wasted. You'll only get out of a battery a little more than 70% of the energy you put in.

A battery is simply a collection of cells joined together. When a battery is new and in perfect condition this fact has little practical effect other than on the charging time. As a battery ages the losses in the individual cells become more pronounced and affect the performance of the battery as a whole.

FUNDAMENTALS OF A CELL

All cells consist of electrodes made from two different materials immersed in an electrolyte. Most commonly the cells used in boat batteries are lead–acid ones.

Electrodes are the sources of the electricity. In each cell there is one positive electrode (the anode) and one negative one (the cathode). Electrolyte is the conducting medium used to link the electrodes. It plays a crucial role in the cell process. In use, one and sometimes both of the plates break down chemically and it is this breakdown that produces an electric potential.

A single cell produces a voltage of about 1–2 V depending on its chemical composition. A battery consists of a number of cells joined one after the other. The voltages of the cells are added together to give the required output voltage.

PRIMARY AND SECONDARY CELLS

There are two kinds of cells – primary and secondary. The primary cell is a once-only device. Its active ingredients are consumed during discharge; you throw it away once the energy has been used up. This is the kind of cell used in torches and portable radios. They are often referred to as 'dry cells' since the electrolyte used is in the form of a paste or gel rather than a free-flowing liquid. This definition is now outdated as many secondary cells are also 'dry'.

In secondary cells the chemical process is reversible. When a proportion of the electricity available has been used (generally about 80% maximum) it's possible to bring the device back to its original condition by pushing an electric current through it in the opposite direction. This is what happens in a car or boat battery.

Cell voltage

A lead–acid secondary battery is so called because its cells are made from plates of lead (or lead compounds) and its electrolyte is sulphuric acid in water. Such a cell produces a PD of about 2 V across its terminals on load. Hence to achieve 12 V, six cells connected in series are needed.

A heavy duty battery, ideal for marine use.

CAPACITY (THE CURTAIN LIFTED)

The capacity of the cell is a measure of its ability to do 'work'. In other words, how much power it can give and for how long. For this reason capacity is usually stated in **ampere/hours.**

Unfortunately there are a variety of ways of stating this. First there is the **20 hour rating** often quoted in technical data. This is found by calculating the current the battery can supply at a constant rate for 20 hours at 25° C without the cell voltage dropping below 1.75 V. For example, a 120 ampere/hour rated battery should be able to supply 6 A for 20 hours when brand new.

A ninety ampere/hour battery should in theory be able to supply a current of up to 90 amps for 1 hour, or 45 for 2 hours, or 3 amps for 30 hours and so on. The further away you get from the 20 hour current figure, the less you can rely on this.

Another way of stating the capacity is becoming more common since it is important for starting engines. This is the **cold cranking capacity** which is obtained by discharging the battery at –18° C at a high current (the cold cranking current) for 30 seconds while maintaining a minimum terminal voltage of 1.2 V per cell. Yet another way is to state the **reserve capacity**. This is how many minutes it takes to discharge the cell to a terminal voltage of 1.75 V at a constant current of 25 A.

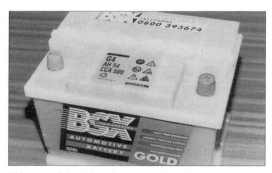

A battery label showing the rating in ampere hours (54) and the cold cranking capacity (500 A).

Both the latter are often stated on the label, with the ampere/hour figure sometimes given as an afterthought on a separate sticker.

Confusing? I'm afraid it is! Information on the battery label can be difficult to follow. This is a 54 AH battery but the figures shown are sometimes the cold cranking ability and reserve capacity. The 'cold cranking' value (in this case 500 A) is more important for a starting battery (the engine handbook will tell you how much current you need for starting). The 'reserve capacity' will give you an idea of the maximum current you can draw from your service batteries.

Actual capacity is largely determined by the surface area of the electrodes in contact with the electrolyte. To increase this area each electrode consists of several linked plates interleaved with, but mechanically separated from, those of the other electrode. The plates can also be made porous, but there are limits to this for structural reasons. Two types of construction are employed to give different properties. Many thin plates may be used, or fewer and thicker ones to withstand more rugged conditions. The choice depends on the anticipated use.

DEEP-DISCHARGE OR HIGH-CURRENT BATTERIES?

Differing demands are placed on batteries by the devices they supply – they may need to supply high short-term currents (e.g., a car battery), or have to produce low currents over long periods.

A car engine takes a current in the order of 200–300 amps to start it, but once running its battery does very little work. The alternator provides the electricity for ignition and other purposes. Within a very short time of driving off, the battery is charged up again and ready for the next start. On a motor vessel the needs may be fairly similar unless, of course, you want power when you moor up.

On a sailing vessel things are bound to be different. Whether at sea, or in harbour, energy is usually taken from the boat's battery when the engine is turned off. Instruments, lights – maybe the autopilot and radar – are all drawing power with none going back. The consequence is that the battery gets heavily discharged when in use. We often expect a quick recharge to work: perhaps just the time taken when entering or leaving harbour under engine; or we run the engine while on a mooring at low revolutions 'just to charge the batteries'.

You will often find a label on a car battery stating that the guarantee is invalidated if the battery is used for marine purposes. Battery manufacturers aren't silly. They know that marine use makes demands which a car battery isn't designed to cope with. Fortunately there are heavy-duty batteries specifically designed for marine use and, although they cost more, are a sound investment, especially if you sail rather than motor most of the time.

ENGINE STARTING

To start the engine you need rather more current on a boat than for a normal petrol car since a diesel engine has a higher compression ratio and thus a greater cranking torque. You need a battery capable of giving a high current (up to 350 A) for short periods. A heavy-duty tractor battery is good for the job and is cheaper than a boat battery

SENSIBLE PRECAUTIONS WITH BATTERIES

Lead–acid batteries can be dangerous if not handled correctly. The electrolyte is acid and corrosive to the skin. A heavily gassing battery can spray out droplets if the plugs are removed. Eye protection is advisable in such cases. The gases produced are highly flammable. A short on a charged battery can cause a fire. So take sensible precautions:

1. Ensure the battery compartment is well ventilated.
2. Fit terminal protectors on the batteries.
3. Install batteries in an acid-proof container.
4. Secure the batteries AND their container to prevent movement.
5. Fit a cover to prevent tools or other metal objects from getting onto them.
6. Fit a battery isolator switch if one is not already fitted.
7. Wear eye protection when working with open batteries.
8. Do not make or break connections to an open battery.
9. Do not use a naked flame near any battery.
10. Keep tools clear of the second terminal when making adjustments at the first.
11. Have a fire extinguisher suitable for electrical fires fitted close to the battery compartment.
12. Use rubber gloves when clearing up any acid spillage.
13. Keep a copy of *First Aid Afloat* by Dr Robert Haworth (published by Fernhurst Books) with your medical kit and read the section on corrosive burn treatment in advance.
14. Include Predsol N eyedrops in your First Aid Kit.

if you want to economise. But it won't cope as well with the mechanical stress demands that a sailing boat makes on it.

Re-charging isn't a problem for a dedicated engine battery since this high-current–short-use type of drain is more easily replaced with short engine running-times.

A word of caution though, if your battery also supplies internal circuits: when the engine is idling it may not be generating sufficient power to charge a low battery properly, even though the 'charging' light is out. This is especially so if much of the generator output is being used by auxiliary circuits particularly at night or in the evening when lights and radios are drawing power. The result can be that the battery gets only a surface charge and gradually loses power. Separate heavy-duty batteries for 'starting the engine' and deep-discharge batteries for 'service' use are a better idea.

TESTING THE BATTERY

With open cell lead–acid batteries a hydro-meter, which measures the relative density or specific gravity of the electrolyte, gives the best indication of condition. The hydrometer consists of a small graduated float inside a glass tube fitted with a rubber squeeze bulb. In use some of the electrolyte is drawn into

USING A HYDROMETER
To measure the Specific Gravity of the
electrolyte in a re-fillable battery:

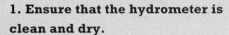

1. Ensure that the hydrometer is
clean and dry.
2. Clean and dry the top of the
battery.
3. Remove the cap from one
battery cell at a time and put
it aside in a safe place.
4. Check that the electrolyte
covers the top of the plates in
each cell to a depth of
approximately 5 mm.
5. If topping up is required the
battery must be left to stand for at
least one hour before you take a
reading.
6. Hold the bulb of the hydrometer
and lower the rubber tube into the
first cell until it touches the top of
the plates.
7. Squeeze the bulb gently but
fully.
8. Slowly relax your hand,
allowing liquid to be drawn into
the bulb.
9. Keeping the hydrometer
vertical, note the reading on the
floating tube.

10. Note if the
electrolyte is dirty or discoloured.
11. Squeeze the bulb again to push
the liquid back into the cell.
12. While still squeezing, gently
withdraw the hydrometer until it is
clear of the electrolyte.
13. Release and squeeze again to
ensure that all the electrolyte has
returned to the cell.
14. Repeat steps 6–13 for each
cell. Replace the stoppers as each
is tested.
15. Compare the readings for each
cell. They should be of the same
value within ten units.
16. Recharge as necessary.
17. After recharging allow to stand
for half an hour, then top up the
electrolyte levels if necessary and
allow to stand for one hour before
re-testing.
18. Dirty or discoloured
electrolyte or a reduced volume
in one cell indicates a cell in poor
condition.

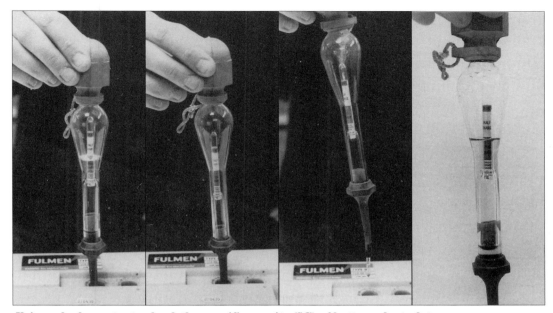

Using a hydrometer to check the specific gravity (SG) of battery electrolyte
1. Put the hydrometer into one of the cells. 2. Squeeze the bulb until enough electrolyte is withdrawn to float the plunger. 3. Take the reading of the electrolyte on the plunger's scale. 4. Here it reads 'Fully charged' – just! Repeat the procedure for each cell in turn.

the tube and the level at which the float settles is calibrated. It works because sulphuric acid is denser than water and the acid concentration varies with the state of charge.

As the cell discharges the acid solution becomes weaker, and it is reconstituted during charging. The hydrometer measures these changes. In a fully charged cell the hydrometer reading should be 1350 (pure water is 1000), while a flat cell shows about 1150. If the reading falls below 1100 the cell may be damaged beyond recall.

Note that both the gases produced during charging burn. They come partially from the breakdown of water, and such cells need chemically pure water adding to them from time to time to restore the loss.

BATTERY METERING

It would be useful to have a simpler means of knowing the battery charge/discharge condition. The easiest way to do this is to have both a voltmeter and an ammeter permanently wired into the system. All large and most medium-sized power vessels have this arrangement. Many yachts under 12 m don't, which is a pity. Neither meter is expensive and each can be added by a competent electrician.

Ammeters

An ammeter indicates the current going into and out of the battery. It usually has a centre zero with a positive deflection indicating charge and a negative one discharge. It works by measuring the voltage drop across a device called a shunt. This is a high thermal capacity resistor which is wired in series with the battery. The choice of shunt depends on the maximum current to be drawn. The ammeter itself, which actually measures the PD across the shunt, does not need to be close to it since the meter current is only a fraction of the total.

Separate meters need to be fitted for each

battery unless a switching arrangement is provided. Effective metering cannot be achieved while batteries are connected in parallel.

So long as the ammeter reads on the positive side once the engine starts running, things should be OK. For this reason many boatbuilders dispense with the meter and provide only an 'ignition warning light'. This light should come on when the starter circuit is made live by turning the key. It goes out when the engine runs, indicating that current is being produced by the alternator but does not tell you how much is going into the battery. This can be important.

Voltmeters

The standing voltage reading should be taken with the battery switch set to each battery in turn. A permanently-installed voltmeter should have a press-to-read switch. It must not be wired permanently across the battery since this will provide a path to discharge it and the battery will go flat.

A voltmeter can be used to tell the condition of the batteries. Immediately after charging a 12 V lead–acid battery, the open circuit between the terminals (i.e., with the battery selector switch set to 'off') should be about 13.8 V. This is the charging voltage. After standing for an hour or so this reading will drop slightly but should still be over 13.0 V. Twelve hours later it should still be at least 12.8 V if no load has been drawn and if the battery is in good condition. A drop to below 12.5 V will often be the first indication that the battery is past its best. It may mean that there is insufficient charge left to operate higher-powered devices such as the starter motor or a radar. If the battery terminal voltage drops below 11.5 V the battery is 'flat' and should be recharged. A drop to below 11.0 V can mean permanent damage.

The changes between 'good' and 'bad' are thus small. To measure these small differences accurately special instruments are

EMERGENCY TREATMENT FOR CORROSIVE CHEMICALS IN THE EYE

If you get any battery acid in your eyes, possibly as a result of a gassing battery, you will feel intense pain. Action should be taken immediately if the eye is to be saved. This is the treatment recommended by Dr Robert Haworth, the author of *First Aid Afloat* (which is also published by Fernhurst Books).

Treatment

1. Hold the eye open and pour copious amounts of clean water over it to dilute and wash away the chemical. Continue until you are sure that the chemical has been washed away.
2. Drop four Predsol N eyedrops into the eye and repeat every four hours.
3. Ask the casualty to close the eye, then cover it with a pad and fix the pad with Sellotape (Scotch Tape).
4. Give two paracetamol for the pain.
5. If the pain is intense, close and cover the good eye in the same way.
6. You must get the casualty to medical treatment as soon as possible if the sight of the eye is to be saved.
7. It may be necessary to issue a PAN-PAN MEDICO message over the emergency channel.

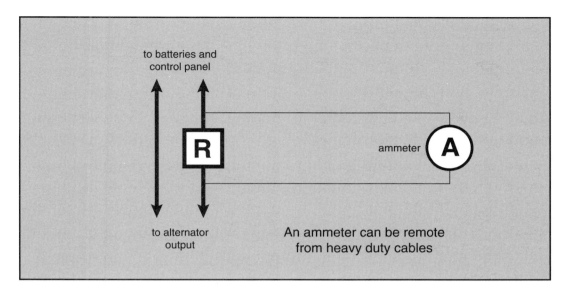

to batteries and
control panel

R

ammeter (A)

to alternator
output

An ammeter can be remote
from heavy duty cables

needed. Such meters have a scale starting at 10 V with a maximum full scale deflection of 15 V. You can get a fair idea of the condition however with an ordinary voltmeter having a 15 V scale. Some modern instruments have a digital readout which helps. Cheap instruments may have a scale inaccuracy of plus or minus 5% however.

SEALED BATTERIES

Modern lead–acid batteries are sometimes called 'sealed for life' and are referred to as 'maintenance free' since they don't need topping up. The gases released are chemically stored in the battery and re-combined to form water. These batteries are not totally sealed and do give off very small quantities of gas, particularly if overcharged. Care over this is essential, since once the gases have been

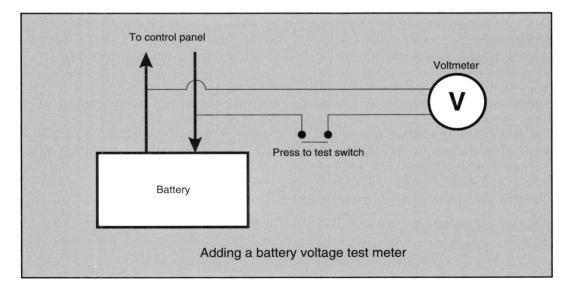

To control panel

Voltmeter

V

Press to test switch

Battery

Adding a battery voltage test meter

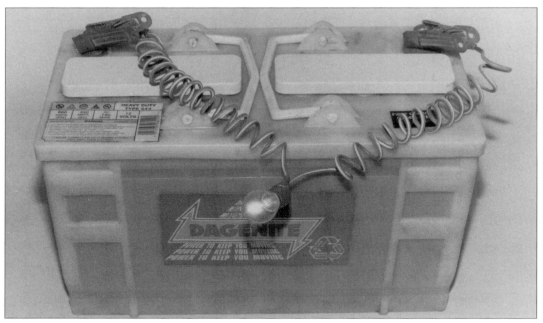

This battery has been trickle-charged and is now discharging steadily through an old bulb.
When repeated several times this may cure minor sulphation problems.

vented they cannot be put back. A hydrometer can't be used on such a battery; instead a voltage check should be carried out on the basis described above.

GASSING

Hydrogen is given off during discharge and oxygen during charging of lead–acid cells, so good ventilation is important. The quantity of gas released is small and generally disperses easily but can accumulate in an enclosed space. Unventilated, under-bunk stowage is just such a space.

A rapid gassing, particularly during charging, is generally evidence of a deteriorating battery (or cell). If all cells gas a lot it may mean that the voltage regulator is not working correctly giving too high a charging current – so get your alternator checked out by an expert. Further evidence of this is heating of the battery case and/or a need to top-up frequently.

SULPHATION

A lead–acid battery must never be allowed to stand for long in a discharged state. Such a situation will do permanent damage to the cells. Lead sulphate is produced every time the battery is discharged but provided it's recharged fairly soon the sulphate breaks down easily. If the battery is allowed to stand in a discharged condition the sulphation becomes more difficult, and eventually impossible, to reverse.

Minor sulphation problems can sometimes be cured by slow charging until the battery gases freely, and then discharging it fully with a steady load before recharging it. This cycle may need to be repeated several times. Use a trickle charger for charging and an old headlamp bulb for discharging. Check the progress frequently since prolonged gassing, even though it pushes off the sulphate, can damage the cell's structure. Unfortunately, even a single cell suffering from serious sulphation means a new battery.

CHARGING RATES AND THEIR EFFECTS

As we mentioned earlier, alternators have control circuits so that they start charging at a fast rate and reduce the charge as the battery takes on charge. Before starting the charging cycle the tops of all plates should be just covered with electrolyte. Do not overfill because the gas produced during charging can then cause the cells to overflow and lose acid.

When an ammeter is fitted it should be checked from time to time while the engine is running. When running the needle should be around the zero mark, or just positive; it should rarely be in the negative area. A negative reading means that more is being drawn from the system than the alternator can supply.

Trickle chargers seldom have any regulation and should be used with care. As soon as the battery starts gassing, stop charging. Charging at too high a rate or for too long will do permanent damage. Correct the electrolyte level again soon after charging. Wait for a while until all gassing has stopped and any trapped gas has had time to escape.

HEAVY-DUTY vs DEEP-DISCHARGE BATTERIES

Heavy-duty batteries can take a much higher charging current than the slow-discharge types (these are sometimes called deep-cycle batteries). The difference between the two is greater than this. Heavy-duty batteries provide a high current for a short time and do not like to be discharged more than about 20%. Deep-discharge batteries are happy to have as much as 55% of their charge taken out so long as it is done slowly. They are quite the best type to use as service batteries and give long life (5 years plus) but they are almost twice the price of heavy-duty ones.

CARE OF YOUR BATTERIES

With a reasonable amount of care you can double the life of your battery. With abuse and neglect you can halve it!

Keep it clean, keep the outside dry and keep the electrolyte level correct. Make sure the terminals are tight and the cables sound. Watch out for leaks and for loose mountings. The life of all batteries is greater if they are discharged only partly. Rigid mounting is important since shock loads resulting from sudden movements can damage the cell structure.

A charged battery loses its charge over time, even when not connected. The loss rate is about 1% per day at an ambient temperature of 15° C. At lower temperatures the self-discharge rate is reduced slightly. Dirty battery tops, particularly in damp conditions, can easily double the rate of loss. So, try to avoid leaving a battery for more than a month without topping up the charge. In the winter, though self-discharge is slower in the colder conditions, it is best to remove all the batteries from the boat and to recharge them from time to time.

Modern battery cases are made from plastics, usually polypropylene. This material, while highly resistant to corrosion and impact damage, can be damaged by heat. Batteries are best kept cool and away from the engine in any event. Damage from hot pipework, or a carelessly used soldering iron, is irreversible.

BLOCKING DIODES

It is always wise to charge a flat battery separately from a fully charged one rather than to leave them connected in parallel. This problem arises when you have two batteries with one dedicated to the engine: if the service battery is flat and put in parallel with the one serving the engine it will bring that down too.

Charging a flat battery in parallel with a fully charged one just doesn't work. The discharged one has a higher resistance so that most of the current flows through the already-charged battery. This means you

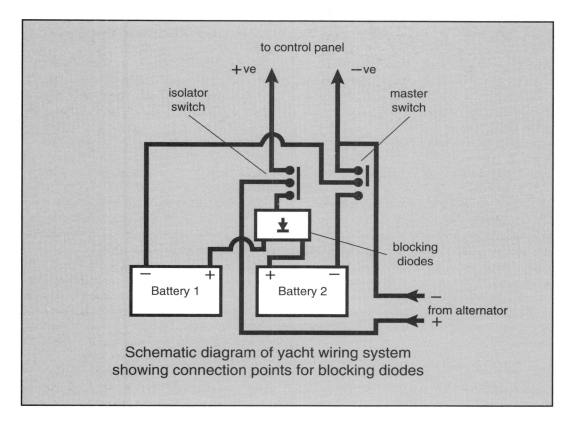

Schematic diagram of yacht wiring system
showing connection points for blocking diodes

need to change the position of the battery control switch to connect the flatter battery to the alternator and charge it separately. Put the switch back to 'both' when the flat battery is charged.

One way to get over this problem is to use blocking diodes. The positive line from the alternator is taken to one terminal (marked 'common' or 'alternator') on the diode block. The positive terminal of each battery is then connected to one of the other terminals. Blocking diodes come in combined units of two, three or four diodes. Diodes allow a current to flow in one direction only; thus each acts as a one-way switch to prevent one battery discharging the other.

However, these devices normally produce a voltage drop (about 0.7 V) across each diode and cannot be used if the alternator output voltage is too low. They also give off

quite a lot of heat and must be mounted where circulating air can disperse this. Some alternators have adjustable voltage taps to get round the voltage drop problem. Fitting diodes is best left to a professional electrician unless you are very experienced at electrical work. He may be able to adjust the alternator to correct for the voltage drop.

SAFETY

Care must be taken when using metal tools on, or near, batteries. A short-circuit can release several kilowatts of energy; enough to melt a screwdriver, burn a chunk out of a spanner or cause a metal watch strap or finger ring to reach red heat in a fraction of a second!

If salt water gets into a lead–acid cell, chlorine gas is given off. This gas is toxic and was the cause of a number of deaths in the

Batteries properly mounted in a plastic battery box.

early days of submarines. Provided filler caps are tight and of the non-spill variety, the risks in a yacht are small. Batteries should always be strapped down tightly in a watertight but open-topped container. This reduces the chances of spilt acid getting into any water that happens to be in the bilges, perhaps from a cracked case.

Sparks from loose terminals, quite apart from causing equipment failure, are a fire hazard so check terminals frequently for condition. Whenever a battery is disconnected both terminals and posts should be cleaned and greased lightly with water-inhibiting grease, such as Vaseline, before replacement.

BATTERY LOCATION

Fit moulded GRP or plastic battery boxes, firmly attached to the boat and with adequate restraints for the contents. These containers should be capable of containing the entire electrolyte from a leaking battery without being more than 75% full. Batteries also need ventilated covers, or at least terminal protectors, if the stowage is open-topped, to avoid risks from dropping tools or other metal objects on them.

In production boats the location of the main batteries will have been determined during the design stage. The ideal position is close to both the alternator and starter motors, and on the centreline of the boat for weight considerations. They should preferably be outside the engine compartment to keep them cool and away from any sparks. They should also be high enough so that a serious leak in the hull will not cause them to flood.

In practice it is difficult to satisfy all these criteria. The closeness to the alternator and starter motor is important due to the high currents that run in their connecting wires. In sailing boats batteries are often fitted under a bunk on the outside of an engine bulkhead. Motor boats more often have batteries in the engine compartment. The vulnerability to the risk of short circuits and sparks makes demands on such an installation's protection.

OTHER SECONDARY BATTERIES

NiFe cells are another type of rechargeable battery which are sometimes found in boats. Ni and Fe are the chemical symbols for nickel and iron – these are the materials from which the electrodes are made. These cells have an output of only 1.34 V, so nine are needed instead of the usual six to produce a 12 V battery.

Though they are much more expensive than lead–acid cells their charge lasts longer, they will put up with being left discharged for long periods and they have a much greater useful life. The state of charge of a NiFe cell is difficult to test since a hydrometer can't be used. The high cost of these cells has precluded their large-scale use, although they did have a surge in popularity just after the Second World War when large numbers of ex-government ones came on the second-hand market. I know one boat which is still fitted with them!

NiCad (nickel–cadmium) batteries are seldom found as a boats main batteries due to the high ratio of cost to adequate output. Like

Modern plastics are used to construct solar panels that are truly flexible.

NiFe cells, they can stand up to more abuse. They are more common at low capacities – in rechargeable torches for example. They should not be used in memory storage devices. Their output stops abruptly when the charge falls below a trigger level which could result in memory loss.

Small rechargeable cells, like those used in fluxgate compasses, clocks and the memories of some fixed instruments, are less liable to cause damage but these, other than in instrument memories, are best removed for the winter. The period during which they'll retain the instrument's memory will be given in the handbook. Make sure that this time is not exceeded. If necessary connect a 12 V battery to the input terminals for a few hours each month during the off-season to reactivate them.

RENEWABLE ENERGY SOURCES

These replenish your battery capacity direct from sun, wind or water power. Renewable energy sources can do a lot to meet the sailboat's electrical energy demands. They will certainly maintain your batteries, extend their life and support security alarms, automatic bilge pumps and other stand-by systems. They will also allow you to overwinter your batteries on board.

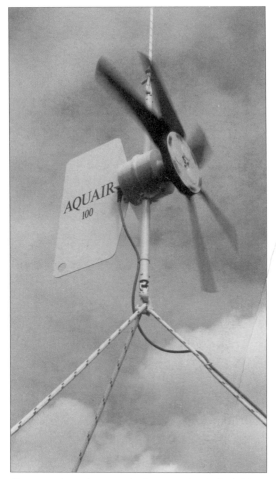

For use at anchor, a wind generator to hoist in the rigging.

Larger systems will support autopilots and other navigation equipment underway and provide useful back-up to alternator charging at anchor, perhaps not eliminating engine running altogether, but greatly reducing it. The savings in engine wear and fuel adding to the satisfaction of being self-sufficient and non-polluting.

Solar panels

Solar panels convert sunlight into electrical energy. The output varies with the intensity of light, but between 4 and 10 Amp/hours each

You get high outputs with windspeeds above 10 knots.

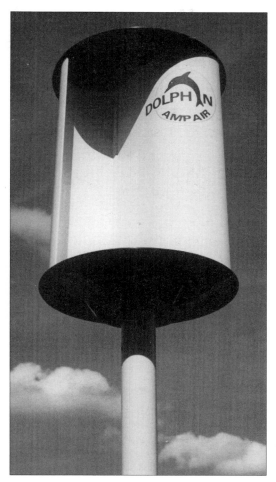

Vertically-mounted wind generators give a much lower output but they are quieter and safer.

day can be generated in the summertime by panels rated from 10 to 30 watts. A small panel will maintain the battery of a moored boat in a healthy condition. This extends battery life and compensates for self-discharge. Some popular panels are constructed without glass, being totally encapsulated in 'high-tech' plastics to produce a truly 'flexible' solar panel.

Wind generators

These come in two types: those having a horizontal axis with a multi-bladed turbine to catch the wind and those having a vertical axis and cylindrical blades. The former is capable of producing high outputs at winds above 10 knots or so. The latter gives a much lower output but is unobtrusive, quiet and safer. The 'fan' variety must be mounted well above head-height since the blades can be lethal in strong winds. In UK coastal waters a daily charge approaching 50 Amp/hours is feasible, increasing to 100 Amp/hours in Force 5 winds.

A dedicated water-powered generator, this underwater unit charges in waterspeeds from 2 knots onwards.

Water turbines

Water turbines are similar in concept to wind turbines but because of the density of the medium (water being a lot denser than air) they can generate worthwhile amounts of electricity at relatively low boatspeeds. A boatspeed of 6 knots can produce a current of 5 A at 12 V. Sailing downwind you would need almost 30 knots of wind to get the same output from a wind generator.

The towed turbine generator offers the simplest system. A gimballed generator is suspended from the pushpit by lanyards. The turbine is towed on a long rope line which transmits the turbine's rotation to the generator shaft. An advantage of this scheme is the conversion of the generator into a wind charger to hoist in the rigging when at anchor.

An alternative generator is totally submerged in use and requires a raising and lowering arrangement for boat operation. Charging down to 2 knots, this system produces the greater output but at a proportionally greater drag level.

The towed turbine generator is ideal for downwind sailing and converts to wind charging at anchor.

4 Crank motors

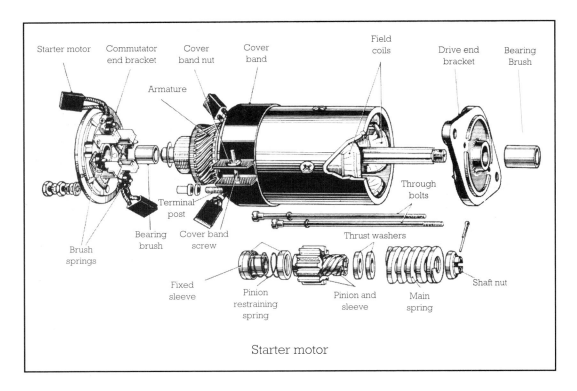

Starter motor · Commutator end bracket · Cover band nut · Cover band · Field coils · Drive end bracket · Bearing Brush · Armature · Terminal post · Bearing brush · Cover band screw · Brush springs · Through bolts · Thrust washers · Fixed sleeve · Pinion restraining spring · Pinion and sleeve · Main spring · Shaft nut

Starter motor

It's not easy to start a marine diesel engine by hand. In practice, the facility isn't provided on many engines over about 25 HP – electric starter motors to crank the engine are the norm.

A starter motor must turn the engine with sufficient speed and power to overcome the cylinder compression and to fire it. Once a diesel engine is running, it doesn't need electricity since combustion takes place through compression ignition, that is, combustion takes place when the pressure in the combustion chamber is sufficient to ignite the fuel–air mixture. A typical compression ratio will be about 23:1, compared with about 9:1 for a petrol engine. So the cranking torque, the energy needed to overcome the

compression, is much higher for a diesel. A crank motor is little different electrically from a generator operating in reverse. A generator converts mechanical energy into electrical energy while a crank motor turns electrical into mechanical energy.

STARTING
A smaller motor can be used only if it comes under load once it is actually turning – a loaded start just wouldn't be possible for a smallish motor. To get around the problem, the starter motor is equipped with a toothed pinion which is mounted on the shaft, but it doesn't actually engage the ring gear on the flywheel. Various ingenious ways of making the pinion then engage the ring gear have

The decompression lever makes starting easier, and hand-cranking possible.

been devised, which all work on the same basic principle.

The most common of the mechanical starters is the bendix drive, often mounted on top of the starter motor. It consists of a toothed pinion which is free to slide along its shaft but must turn with it. When the motor spins, inertia causes the pinion to run, along splines or a coarse thread cut in the shaft, against the pressure of a light spring, until it engages the teeth on the flywheel ring and starts that turning. As soon as the engine fires and the key is released the starter motor slows down. The speed of the flywheel then exceeds that of the pinion which causes this to disengage and run back to its original position, assisted by the spring. Once released, the pinion is held clear by the spring pressure.

STARTER PROBLEMS

Trouble with the starter mechanism isn't that common. Failure to engage, or a 'clunk'

heard as it tries to engage, is most usually due to a supply voltage problem. This happens if insufficient power is available to overcome the static torque. A starter motor often needs 300 amps or more to turn the engine, so check the battery condition first. If the engine battery is in good condition it is worth checking all the connections before going any further. Isolate the battery at the switch before you do this.

The pinion does sometimes stick on the shaft and fail to engage fully. This is caused by dust in the lubricant and is more common on road vehicles. Routine maintenance should prevent it. Cleaning the assembly with a little diesel fuel and then lubricating it with light oil will do the trick if this does happen – you may well have to remove the starter motor to do this. Failure to deal quickly with the problem can cause a tooth or teeth on the pinion to wear sufficiently to cause jamming or sticking. In such cases the sprocket must be

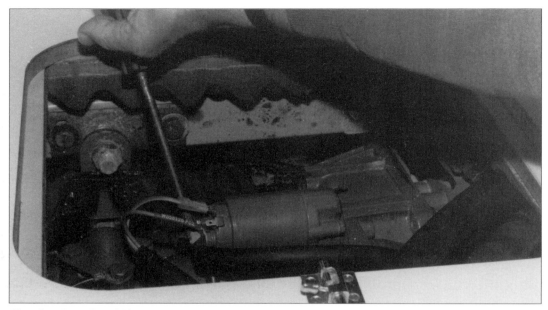

Shorting the solenoid in an emergency.

replaced before it does damage by breaking a tooth on the flywheel. Rarer still is a broken spring resulting in the pinion failing to disengage fully. The symptom is an expensive grinding noise!

SOLENOID CONTROL

Most systems use the ignition key to operate a magnetic switch, called a solenoid, to connect the power to the starter motor. In a solenoid a small current is used to energise a coil-magnet which pulls in a metal core, closing a high-current switch. This reduces the length of the heavy-duty cables needed to carry the high starter motor currents, and reduces the power losses in them.

Solenoids, themselves, sometimes give trouble. Locate the device (it's usually close to, or mounted on, the starter motor) and see if it can be operated manually (a manual mechanical over-ride is sometimes fitted to older engines in the form of a rubber-covered plunger joined to the core). Use this if the coil has become an open circuit. Keep your body and all clothing well clear of moving parts and

take great care while doing this. Depress the plunger firmly to make the connection. Release the plunger as soon as the engine fires.

If there is no mechanical over-ride it may be possible to bridge the contacts. If you have to do this, use a large screwdriver. Take care not to touch anything with the tool other than the actual contacts. Keep all your clothing well clear of the flywheel. Be firm and positive, expect a big spark and don't let it make you jump.

 Bridging the solenoid is an extreme measure. It should only be done as a last resort and with extreme caution. I include it only because you may be forced into it at sea.

GETTING ROUND THE PROBLEM OF LOW BATTERY VOLTAGE

Keeping the key turned and winding the engine for long periods will do more harm

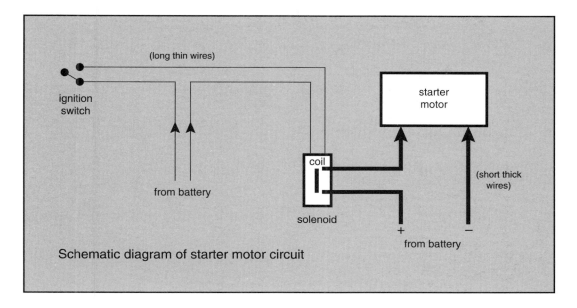

Schematic diagram of starter motor circuit

than good if the motor engages but only turns slowly. Fifteen to twenty seconds is the maximum time the starter should be engaged continuously. Any longer than that and you can damage the crank motor. The high current drain will quickly flatten a low battery too.

Try letting the engine stand after cranking for a short while. This will allow the battery to recover a bit while allowing the warmth created during the initial cranking to raise the cylinder temperature. At the next attempt the engine may start.

The only other solutions are to reduce the *required* energy input or increase the *actual* input. There are several ways of achieving either or both of these.

A pre-heater, sometimes called a 'glow-plug', can be effective. A glow-plug was often provided on older engines, either with its own spring-loaded switch or one incorporated into the ignition switch. A pre-heater takes a lot less power than the crank motor and makes starting a lot easier.

Sometimes a decompression lever is fitted. In the decompressed position the engine will turn faster, under a reduced load. Flick the lever back when full speed has been reached and the engine should fire. If this works don't be in a hurry to throttle back. Let the engine run fast for a few minutes and then gently reduce the revolutions to a fast idle (about 1000–1200 rpm).

Another option, if your service batteries are fully charged, is to use them instead of – or as well as – the engine batteries. If this facility is not available consider altering the wiring to provide it.

Proprietary cold-start sprays, which contain neat alcohol, can be sprayed into the air intakes for a second or two as the engine is turned on compression. This improves ignition and will often bring a reluctant engine to life. Be sparing with the spray because too much can thin the oil and/or cause too rapid combustion, either of which may damage the engine. If the spray is needed frequently, it indicates an engine in poor condition.

A cold engine can take between three and four times as much energy to start as a warm one. With an indirectly-heated system and no pre-heater it is worth draining out most of the fresh water and replacing it with kettles of hot water to raise the cylinder temperature. Don't

Using jump leads to start your engine

You can jump start your boat in the same way as you would a car.

1. Borrow a fully-charged battery.
2. Attach the negative to the negative.
3. THEN attach the positive to the positive.
4. Start the engine.
5. Disconnect the positive leads at both ends.
6. Then disconnect the negative leads, and remove the borrowed battery.

The reason for connecting and disconnecting the leads in the order suggested, is to try to minimise the dangers of the positive lead arcing out if it were to be dropped.

forget to replace the anti-freeze!

JUMP LEADS

On a pontoon berth you may be able to use jump leads from a good battery on a nearby boat. They must be of good quality and fairly short so you will probably have to take the good battery aboard and stand it beside your own (long jump leads introduce too great a voltage drop). The vessel loaning the battery must have a second battery. As an added precaution it should have its engine run up to operating temperature. But stop the engine before removing the first battery.

Take care when making the battery connections. Clip on one lead at a time: connect the negative terminal of the borrowed battery to the negative terminal of your battery, then connect the two positive terminals in the same way, avoiding contact with any nearby metal. To remove the leads, reverse the sequence.

Don't disconnect your own battery from the system when using jump leads since you may damage your alternator if you try to reconnect it with the engine running.

HAND CRANKING

I have rarely been able to start a modern diesel engine by hand but it can be done. If a handle facility is available, and the handle will turn full circle, try it. It has been known for an engine to be installed in such a way that the handle will not turn full circle. The pre-heater and decompression tips mentioned above will make hand starting a lot easier. The engine may kick back as it fires, so hold the handle carefully with thumb and fingers all on the same side.

STARTING A DIESEL ENGINE BY HAND

1. Make sure the engine is out of gear.
2. Locate your starting handle.
3. If a decompression lever is fitted, set it to decompress.
4. Check that the handle will turn full circle when engaged.
5. Turn on the fuel supply tap.
6. Set the battery switch to '1' or 'both'. You must have a battery connected to protect the alternator if and when the engine starts.
7. Have some spray starting-aid handy.
8. Engage the handle with the hand grip at about two o'clock or ten o'clock, depending on the direction of rotation. Most engines turn clockwise when viewed from the cranking end but the handle will only engage when turned in the correct direction.
9. Grasp the handle with all your fingers and your thumb on the same side. This will save your thumb if the engine kicks back.
10. Turn the engine over slowly at least two turns to check that it's free, to circulate some oil and to get some fuel into the cylinders.
11. Get ready for the starting attempt.

Keep your thumb on the same side as your fingers when hand cranking or you'll find yourself a medical emergency.

12. Have an assistant ready to close the decompression lever on your word.
13. Swing the handle and try to get the engine rotating fast.
14. When you can go no faster tell your assistant to operate the compression lever.
15. Keep turning if possible until the engine fires.
16. If it has not fired, stop for breath!
17. Pour a kettle of hot, but not boiling, water over the fuel pump.
18. Decompress again.
19. Repeat steps 12–16, BUT as soon as the engine is compressed have your assistant squirt 'Damp-Start' or 'Easystart' into the air intake for 1–2 seconds only.
20. If it now won't fire, wait ten minutes and try steps 12–19 again.
21. If it still doesn't start, then it probably won't!

5 Distribution & control

The alternator output will go to the batteries via the selector switch and any blocking diodes that may be fitted. It also goes to the main control panel. The service battery supplies the main distribution or control panel through this switch when the alternator has no output. All the boat's consumer circuits other than engine starting circuit will go via this panel. Some boats have only one panel combining the functions of distribution and control. Others have a main distribution panel which supplies supplementary control panels. This latter system is far better but is more costly to install and so is unlikely to be found on a production yacht.

MASTER SWITCHES

The battery supply is controlled by the selector switch, allowing more than one service battery to be fitted. Either one or both can be used as required. Thick wires link the alternator and batteries to the control panel through this switch, and all the current used in the boat passes through these wires. Fusing

would not be effective protection because of the high transient currents involved.

An isolator switch in the other side of the supply makes it possible to disconnect the batteries completely in the event of a short-circuit or a wiring fire. It also reduces leakage risks when the boat is left unattended.

RING MAIN OR BRANCHED?

In domestic wiring a ring main is favoured with each supply wire going from the distribution box right round the system and back. While both economical and effective ashore, this system is not appropriate for boats. Houses work on alternating current, boats on direct current. In a motor vehicle, which also works on direct current, the return path from most components is made via the body of the vehicle. This is only possible because the vehicle is made of metal and is insulated from earth by its tyres.

Boats cannot use such a system. A DC ring main would set up magnetic fields which

These thick cables link the battery to the control panel.

The battery isolator switch is the T-shaped one to the left of the round selector switch.

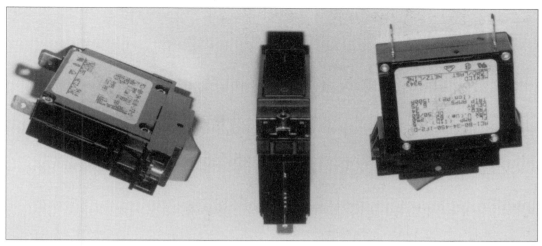

CBEs (Circuit Breakers for Equipment)

could interfere to a dangerous extent with the VHF, compass and other instruments. Using the hull of a metal boat would allow transient currents to be set up which would eat away at, and eventually sink, the vessel. Boats are thus best wired using a pair of wires for each service (called spurs), running out from the distribution panel like the branches of a tree. A pair of adjacent parallel wires carry the outgoing and return current to each component. Thus the currents are equal but flow in opposite directions, and most of the magnetic fields that are generated are cancelled out.

The ideal is to have separate spurs for each area in the boat, with sub-spurs for each separate item, enabling faults to be isolated more easily. The extra cost of sub-control points makes this rare except on very large boats. However it is worth considering if you are having a boat built or fitted-out for you.

CIRCUIT BREAKERS

Each spur circuit must be protected by a fuse or 'circuit breaker' (CBEs as they are called: Circuit Breakers for Equipment). Each power-consuming component should be protected by a switch or a switched circuit breaker. CBEs are available in discrete steps from

1 amp up to about 100 amps. They are very rapid and precise in operation.

These devices use magnetism or temperature, or a combination of the two, to open switch contacts and break the connection. Thermal-only trips should be used where transient currents are likely to be present. Magnetic-solenoid trips will operate almost instantly on any overload.

Specialist circuit breaker manufacturers can supply CBEs in a variety of configurations to suit customer requirements. Magnetic devices that will trip out at 30% above the operating current in a few milliseconds are available. They are capable of withstanding transient currents of up to 100 times the maximum operating current without damage. These devices are also salt water resistant and will trip even when the switch is forcibly held in the 'on' position, and so providing excellent protection.

FUSES

Fuses also blow at maximum current values. They are nowhere near as precise as a circuit breaker and are slow to respond. 'Slow blow' and 'quick blow' fuses are, however, available for special applications. All fuses are triggered by temperature and are destroyed by it.

The time taken to blow a fuse varies not only with design but also with both the magnitude of the overload and its rise time. In simple terms this means that potentially dangerous, damaging currents of up to twice the operating current or more may take some time to blow a fuse so it gives only partial protection. This is a major drawback and the fuse cannot protect sensitive modern equipment. Furthermore, a replacement fuse may not re-blow immediately – this makes it possible to restore a circuit without actually curing the fault.

Electrical installation regulations now require circuit breakers to be fitted to all new domestic systems. Fire on a boat is potentially more life-threatening than in the home, quite apart from the damage done to equipment, so it makes sense to use them aboard too.

SWITCHES

The control panel needs a switch for each circuit, either in addition to – or incorporated in – a circuit-overload device. Use low voltage DC switches, which are different from those used in high voltage AC applications: DC switches invariably carry and switch higher currents than their domestic AC equivalents. In addition DC supplies increase the level of sparking on make-and-break contacts, and so increasing the rate of contact pitting.

The rating of a switch is generally quoted in terms of operating AC or DC voltage, and its current-handling capacity. The choice of any particular switch should always be based on the maximum possible current that may flow in the circuit.

This current can be easily calculated by adding up the rated wattage of each item it supplies and dividing this sum by the supply voltage. For example: 3 x 10 watt filament lamps and 2 x 21 watt fluorescent lamps would give a total wattage of 72 watts. In a 12 V system this would mean a current of 72/12 = 6 amps, requiring at least a 6 A/12 V

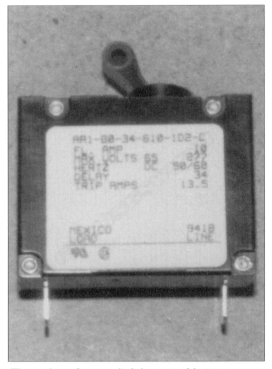

The rating of any switch is quoted in terms of its AC or DC operating voltage and its current-handling capacity.

switch. Even if you never intend to switch all these lights on at once you should allow for that possibility.

Indicators

Each circuit-controlling device should be clearly labelled so that anyone can operate the appropriate switch without having to ask for instructions. Many control panels have illuminated indicators (either LED or filament) to show which circuits are in use. With push button switches this is perhaps necessary; with lever switches less so. Personally, I would rather not have lights: they can be an irritant during night-sailing and they draw part of your precious power. Rocker switches are preferable. They need to be clearly labelled so that they can be read in subdued light. 'Visirocker' CBEs, with their fluorescent

Different cable types.

'on' segments, are a great leap forward in this respect.

WIRING SIZE RULE

Just as switches and fuses must be able to carry their working loads, so too must the wiring. The correct wire size depends on both the current and the loop length. A voltage drop over the total length of more than 5% of the supply voltage isn't acceptable. The table shows the voltage loss per metre for different cable sizes at the maximum operating current. This isn't the general way of rating wire but it is a useful and practical one.

To choose which wire size to use for any job, calculate the current it will have to carry and find the appropriate row. Using a calculator, multiply the volts drop figure given in column six by the loop length in metres to the furthest appliance (that is the length of the cable pair times two). The answer must be less than 0.6 V for a 12 V system or 1.2 V for a 24 V one.

Wire types

There is a lot more to the choice of wire than the size of the conductor. The table lists only those wires which are multi-stranded, because single-strand wire has no place on a boat. Boats move violently, and the wiring will always need to flex without breaking.

TABLE OF WIRE SIZES FOR INTERNAL BOAT WIRING

Voltage drop per metre for standard wire sizes

1	2	3	4	5	6
Cable Size	Core diameter mm (approx.)	Cross sectional area mm^2	Resistance Ohms/m	@ Amps (max. op. rate)	Volts Drop/m @ 20° C
14/0.25	0.90	0.70	0.00453	6.00	0.0272
14/0.30	1.15	1.00	0.00215	8.75	0.0188
19/0.30	1.30	1.35	0.00118	11.75	0.0139
21/0.30	1.40	1.50	0.000980	12.75	0.0125
28/0.30	1.60	2.00	0.000537	17.50	0.0094
50/0.25	1.78	2.50	0.000375	20.00	0.0075
44/0.30	1.95	3.00	0.000218	27.50	0.0060
56/0.30	2.26	4.00	0.000157	30.00	0.0047
65/0.30	2.40	4.50	0.000117	35.00	0.0041
84/0.30	2.75	6.00	0.0000738	42.00	0.0031
97/0.30	3.00	7.00	0.0000540	50.00	0.0027
120/0.30	3.30	8.50	0.0000366	60.00	0.0022
37/0.90	5.64	25.00	0.0000045	170.00	0.000762
61/0.90	7.10	40.00	0.0000015	300.00	0.000462
61/1.13	8.75	60.00	0.0000007	415.00	0.000293

NOTES:

1. The core diameter is included to enable users to identify actual cables. This identification will be approximate only. If in doubt use the next size up.
2. Since the voltage drop is proportional to the current, it's a simple matter to calculate the loss at current values below the maximum. e.g. a 14/0.25 wire carrying 3 A would have a drop of 0.0136 V/m.
3. Column 6 gives the volts drop over 1 m of wire at 20° C at the current shown in column 5. Multiply the column 6 figure by the loop length to find the total volts drop.

Applying $P = I^2 \times R$ will show the power loss to be 0.16 W/m in smaller sizes falling to 0.12 W/m in the largest. This gives a constant temperature rise for all wires at maximum operating current. The figures in the table on page 48 apply to a single cored conductor only. For twin-cored cables the figures in column 5 must be reduced by 15%. This is due to the reduced rate of heat loss in multi-cored cables. If in doubt a larger core size should be used.

In the United States of America wires are coded under a system called the American Wire Gauge. This system assigns a number to each core cross-sectional area. For convenience the following table gives the nearest equivalent AWG Numbers in relation to some more commonly used wire sizes in the UK.

CONVERSION TABLE
BETWEEN UK AND US WIRE SIZES

UK Wires (core area mm^2)	1.0	1.5	2.5	4.0	6.0	10	16	25	35	50	70
AWG No.	18	16	14	12	10	8	6	4	2	0	00

Notes
For AC utility mains supply (including shore-power) the voltages, frequencies and wiring colour coding and are different between the US and UK

Single Phase	American	European
Voltage	110 V	230 V
Frequency	60 Hz	50 Hz

Colour		
Live	Black	Brown
Neutral	White	Blue
Earth	Green	Green with Yellow stripes

6 Additions & mains power

An extra light can be connected to an existing circuit without difficulty provided the 'wiring rule' allows it. Adding a new instrument is a little more complicated. On a generously-built boat you will often find spare circuits provided, or at least spare current limiters and switches. But more often than not, you will have to add them yourself.

PROVIDING EXTRA OUTLETS

When no spare circuits are provided it is best to add a small sub-panel with several separate outlets. This creates some extra

SOLDERING A WIRE TO A TERMINAL

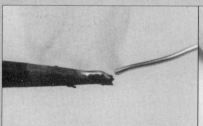

1. First heat the iron until solder flows freely when touched with the solder wire.

2. Strip sbout 1 cm of insulation from the wire to be soldered.

3. Patent cable strippers are more expensive but make the job easier.

7. Now tin the terminal. Hold the soldering iron against it to heat it up.

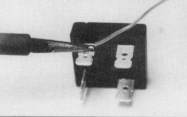

8. Now apply solder to the terminal close to the iron. Heat in the terminal will cause the solder to flow.

9. The solder should flow freely over the terminal coating it evenly.

Panels like these allow you to add extra circuits as you need them.

spare capacity so that you won't have to add more haphazard wiring the next time you fit an item. Blank panels, containing six or more outlets, can be purchased. These are easier to install than a DIY job and a lot neater.

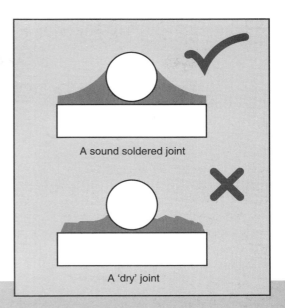

A sound soldered joint

A 'dry' joint

4. The uncovered wire strands will splay out.

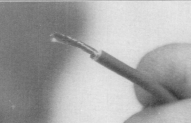

5. Twist the strands together using your fingers.

6. Now tin the wire. Hold it against the hot iron and apply solder to the iron.

10. Hold the iron against the tinned terminal and place the wire against the terminal too. The solder on each will melt and flow together.

11. Remove the iron and hold the wire and terminal still until the solder sets (a few seconds will be all that's needed).

12. Examine the joint carefully. The solder should be bright, shiny and smooth. The joint on the right is 'dry'. It will have a high resistance and could break free.

HOW TO SOLDER

1. Using a low-voltage electric soldering iron

Use resin flux cored solder wire for all electrical joints: ask for this when you buy it. Remove about 10 mm of insulation from the end of the wire using patent wire strippers. If you are soldering old wire make sure it is clean and free from grease. Remove any hard black or powdery, reddish-brown material: this is oxide and will not take solder. Connect the soldering iron to a good battery. (If in doubt, run the engine to keep it charged.) While the iron is warming up clean the tip using a wire brush until bright metal is visible. If the tip is pitted, use a small file and remove some of the metal to level it off. Apply the end of the solder wire to the tip. It should melt instantly and flow, covering the bright metal with a silvery coat.

Some smoke is to be expected. If the solder does not melt straight away, the iron is not hot enough. Wait a few moments and try again. This is called tinning the iron and is essential for good joints.

Once the solder flows easily, wipe off the surplus with a clean rag. Old cotton towelling works best. Now hold the wire to be soldered against the hot tip and apply a little more solder between tip and wire. The solder should melt and flow onto the wire. As soon as this happens remove the heat. If you get a bubble of solder on the wire shake it off while it is still liquid.

Clean the tip of surplus solder again and apply it to the terminal to be connected and tin this in the same way as you did the wire. Next wrap the wire round the terminal to form a mechanical joint. (Some terminals have a small hole in them through which the wire can be passed.) Apply the tip of the iron again to this joint and the solder should flow

---

Modular systems – which allow the DIY fitter to add any number of extra circuits – are preferable. Blanks are available so that the shells can be fitted one at a time. Additional circuit breakers can then be snapped in where they are needed. This saves initial costs while providing for later expansion.

REPLACING A CONTROL PANEL

Before cutting any holes in a panel be sure you are not going to damage either the panel

FITTING A 12 V LIGHTER SOCKET

Fitting a 12 V lighter socket. Drill out the shape inside an outline drawn on masking tape.

Cut to 'join up' the drill holes.

between them completing the electrical path. You may need to apply a little more solder to get the flow going but be sparing; the less solder used the better. Don't take too long over this or the wire's insulation will start to melt!

2. Using a directly-heated gas soldering iron

This type of soldering iron has no built-in temperature control. It has its own gas source from a small gas canister that fits on it. Follow the manufacturer's instructions carefully. Clean the bit before lighting, then adjust the gas and air mixture control until the flame is pale blue and almost invisible. If the flame spreads round the tip reduce the gas flow a little until it only just reaches. Start tinning early so that melted flux keeps the tip clean. Tin the tip and wire as before. Avoid getting the solder wire into the flame or you

will waste a lot of it.

When applying this type of iron to the wire, or to the mechanical joint, be careful where the flame goes. It is almost invisible and could set alight adjacent wires – or worse!

3. Indirectly gas-heated soldering irons

These irons are larger and must be heated using the gas cooker. They are only useful for soldering heavy electrical joints, or for plumbing jobs, when a large heat reservoir is needed. Heat control is difficult and needs practice. The iron is at the right temperature when solder applied to it runs freely without the flux burning into ash. If it is too hot the flux goes to smoke and ash immediately; too cool and the solder is slow to coat the surface and has a dull, crusty appearance.

or things fitted behind it. You will need a keyhole saw, or a rotary saw in a cordless drill. The rotary saw will do the job best and it takes less elbow grease.

An alternative way to remove the waste is to drill a series of small holes round the inside

of the marked line, push out the waste piece and then clean up the hole with a rasp. This is a slower but still effective method and with care can be as neat as sawing. When starting from scratch chose a panel suitable for the space available. Make sure there is sufficient

Clean up with a file.

Fit the socket.

Making an ammeter/voltmeter readout panel

1. Make a template to suit the instrument to be fitted.

2. Lay the template on the panel material and mark the cut-out areas.

3. Drill a ring of holes inside each cut-out area, close to the edge and right round.

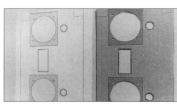

4. Punch out the cut-outs and clean up the edges with a file.

5. The finished panel.

6. Bolt the instrument in place and connect up.

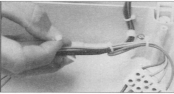

7. Connect the instrument wiring to the loom using terminal blocks (all brass connectors).

8. Bundle the wires together and secure using tie wraps to reduce future vibration damage.

9. Remove surplus wrap with side cutters.

10. Strain relief glands are used if the unit is to be moved from place to place.

11. As the nut is tightened, the cable is gripped.

12. The finished panel bolted into place – a neat job!

REPLACING A CONTROL PANEL

1. Temporarily fit all the components to the panel and measure or calculate the smallest hole needed to fit it into.

2. Offer up the new control panel and check there will be sufficient material left to hold the fixing screws and sufficient space behind it for the new components.

3. If fitting an additional or new size of panel cut out the outline in cardboard first and make sure the assembled new panel fits in it. Offer the cardboard template up to the chosen position and check that all is correct.

4. Cover the approximate positions of each cut with masking tape.

5. Mark the cut-out area on this tape with a water-based felt pen.

6. Drill a pilot hole in the waste area, close to but not overlapping the marked line and large enough to insert the keyhole saw.

7. Work from the outward facing surface of the panel to preserve the edges.

8. Now cut outwards towards the line at a shallow angle and work the saw round just inside the line until the waste can be removed.

9. Remove the tape and finish the edges with sandpaper, then clear up the sawdust.

10. Next offer the assembled switch panel up to the hole (the right way up!) and make sure it fits.

11. Once satisfied that it is correctly positioned, mark the fixing holes, then drill these and fix the panel in place.

---

space for the connections behind the chosen position before starting.

WIRING THE SUB-PANEL

Identify the two supply wires carrying the panel current supply. Disconnect the battery before changing these connections. Run one of these wires to the negative busbar on the original master panel. (The busbar is the thick copper strip connected in common to all the switches.) Transfer the negative supply wire to the negative busbar connected to all the new circuit breakers. Transfer the other supply wire to the positive distribution block on the new panel. Then transfer all the original circuits in turn to the new panel.

Finally check all the transferred circuits individually before the panel is replaced.

The feed to the original panel must be able to carry any extra load you are going to put on the new panel. Otherwise you may need to replace the supply cables direct from the battery. Use good quality new wire of the right size for the job and make the battery connections using soldered or crimped terminals fitted under the clamping nuts.

Fit an in-line fuse between the battery and any new sub-panel to provide separate protection. Its rating should be sufficient for the total panel demand. A panel with 2 x 10 A and 2 x 5 A outlets will thus need fusing at 30 A. The wire should be 56/0.3 cable.

REMOVING INSULATION FROM WIRES

Patent cable strippers

These special tools work by gripping the insulation on a single-core cable before allowing cutting jaws to nip into it. The cutter will go through the insulation but not the wire strands inside. With further pressure it will pull the cut insulation clear of the wire end. At the cost of a few pounds they'll do a good job every time. Even professional electricians are starting to use them.

They are not suitable for removing the outer sheath on multi-cored cables. For this purpose a sharp knife should be used as follows:

1. Work out the amount of sheath to be removed. The less removed the better in most cases.
2. Take the knife and nick the sheath right round the cable but don't cut through it.
3. Bend the sheath over sharply at the nick and the sheath should continue to split away until through.
4. If it doesn't part easily, use the knife again gently.
5. Continue bending in different directions until the sheath is free all round.
6. Straighten the cable and pull the

Connections to busbars may be soldered or screwed. If you want to solder the joints you will need a good heavy-duty soldering iron which can be heated on the gas cooker unless you have a mains supply available. Better still is to try and make the links ashore before taking the new panel aboard.

Alternatively a small gas-operated blow-

Stripping the end of a wire using side-cutting pliers

 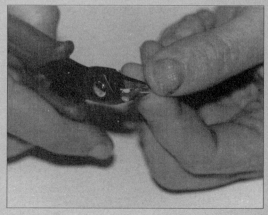

Use gentle pressure while rotating the wire to crease the insulation.

severed sheath from the ends of the wires.

7. If it is reluctant to come away, put the cable on a flat surface and gently score a cut along the length from the nick point to the end.

8. It should now be possible to peel away the unwanted part of the sheath.

To remove the insulation from the individual wires with the stripper:

1. Feed the end of each insulated wire in turn, lengthways, into the jaws of the stripper. Some have graduated marks to get the exact length while others have a stop to give a pre-set length.

2. Squeeze the hand grips gently until the gripper jaws grasp the wire.

3. Continue to squeeze until the cutters nick the insulation.

4. Further squeezing will then withdraw the cutting blades into the tool pulling the waste insulation free of the end.

5. Repeat the operation for each wire to be stripped.

Note: Some versions of the tool have a setting adjustment for different wire sizes but most are self-adjusting.

torch will do the job. If you use a blowtorch take great care against starting a fire. Small 12 V soldering irons are not suitable since they are unable to provide sufficient heat fast enough and will produce what is called a dry joint. This can look fine but will cause a voltage drop, overheat and may start a fire.

Unless you are justifiably confident of your soldering ability it is best to get a professional to do the job for you.

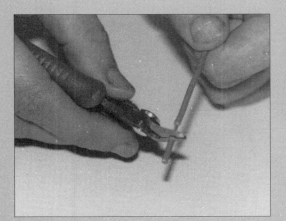
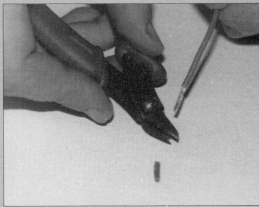

Then, still applying gentle pressure (or you'll cut the core) pull the two apart.

REMOVING AND REPLACING A HEAD LINING TO GET TO THE WIRING BEHIND IT

A. Panel head linings

Many production yachts have fabric-coated plywood panels as head linings. They can be removed easily and almost as easily replaced as follows:

1. Remove any hardwood trim strips, identifying each with a label.
2. Stow the screws in a safe place for re-fixing.
3. Make sure the label markings will identify the location of each piece.
4. With short lengths of masking tape bridge each panel to the next.
5. Label the panels and note their positions on a paper diagram.
6. If only one panel needs to be removed bridge that and adjoining panels only with the masking tape lengths.
7. Draw a line across each bridge with a soft pencil.
8. Label each tape strip at both ends and cut through them between the panels. When the panel is replaced the pencil lines and labels will ensure correct positioning.
9. Remove the screws holding each panel in turn, saving the screws as before. Having an assistant makes panel removal and replacement much easier.
10. When replacing panels work from one end of the deckhead.
11. Secure each panel with the minimum of screws until sure all are positioned correctly.
12. Fit the remaining screws and tighten them all.
13. Remove the tapes.
14. Fit the trim strips in order.

B. Fabric head linings

Some boats (particularly racing yachts) have fabric liners rather than wooden ones to reduce weight. Some of these snap into place and can only be removed by destructive means. Others have blind fastenings which are hidden behind trim strips as above. Some will pop out if pressed in the right places. If you have fabric linings you will have to investigate, but the use of masking tape to locate panels still applies.

INSTALLING NEW EQUIPMENT

In choosing the location think about ease of use and about protection.

- Instruments marked, 'splashproof', should never be fitted where spray can fall on them.
- Kit destined for an exposed location must be designed for the purpose.
- Radar will be difficult or impossible to use if sunlight falls directly on the screen; on the other hand, an instrument that needs to be read from the cockpit must be fitted so that it can be seen from there.

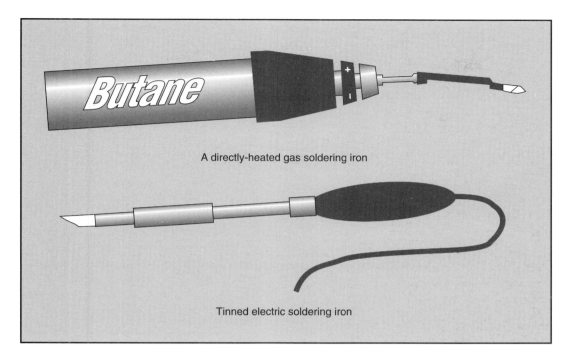

A directly-heated gas soldering iron

Tinned electric soldering iron

INTERFERENCE

Many modern instruments emit radio frequency waves which may cause interaction problems with other bits of kit. A simple way to check on this possibility with a new item is to wire it temporarily first. Make sure you lay the wires where you expect them to finish up but don't fix them down or drill any holes yet. Now switch on and see if the new equipment causes any problems with existing items or is affected by old ones. If all is well you can complete the fitting with confidence. If not, try moving the new item about to see if that helps.

The problems can be two-way. For example, your Decca/Loran and GPS can interfere with the VHF radio producing noise, while a VHF on transmit can cause loss of position on either instrument.

Computers are notorious sources of radiated interference and you may have more of these on the boat than you think: all position-plotting devices contain them. Physical separation helps a lot but may not be practicable round a crowded chart table.

Don't confuse poor battery condition with genuine interference. The symptoms are often very similar, but charging the batteries fully before doing the checks should prevent this mistake.

Screening

An alternative is to use screened cables which can reduce interference altogether. Suppressors can be fitted on supply lines, but they will only prevent interference received via the power supply: they won't help much against radiated interference. In-line suppressors are often rings of ferrite, a highly efficient magnetic material, through which a few turns of the supply cable are wound. For maximum benefit the rings should be fitted as close to the instrument as possible.

Screening the cable means enclosing it in a wire mesh sleeve, or a metal tube, which is earthed. Screened cable is available from most good electronics shops. The earthing may need to be at frequent intervals, sometimes as close as half a metre.

AVAILABLE POWER

It is easy to keep adding extra gadgets to your boat and forget about the power requirements. Power is one of your finite resources. Take care to avoid over-demand. If the average load exceeds the generator output you'll have a problem: the batteries will never get fully charged and their lives will be shortened. You'll find yourself running the engine more and more, even under sail, to supply the increased demand. The solution is an expensive one: a bigger generator and probably bigger batteries.

EARTHING AND EARTH-BONDING

Skin fittings, the keel, the engine, pumps and the propeller are normally metal and these metals may all be different. Since they are linked by an electrolyte – sea water – they form cells which produce electricity. As in any cell, the anode decomposes in time. In some instances this time can be surprisingly short.

On large ships a permanent DC potential is applied to all metal fittings so that they become in effect cathodes. This solution is impractical on a small boat so an alternative strategy has been devised.

Zinc is high up on the galvanic table. So a piece of zinc connected to each metal item in contact with the water will act as an anode, and this will then be the only thing that wastes away.

The lump of zinc is called the sacrificial anode. It is bolted to the outside of the hull in contact with the sea. Seacocks and the rest are bonded internally to it. Under the electrolytic action it slowly wastes away but is cheaper than the items it protects and can be replaced relatively easily. In practice, the bonding links must be kept short (2–3 m) and be thick enough to avoid voltage drops in themselves. On larger boats, it's often more effective to fit several anodes. Sometimes a separate anode is fitted on the propeller shaft, both because this is an expensive item, and also because the shaft may not be in electrical contact with the other underwater metals. The bonding links are a vital part of the system and should be regarded as being more important than any other wiring.

SHORE SUPPLIES

Many boats are fitted with a 240 V circuit that can be plugged into a mains supply source in a marina berth. This gives several benefits: you can charge the batteries, use an electric kettle and hair dryer, watch TV (if you must!) and run a heater. Mains-operated, low-output greenhouse-type heaters can be particularly useful since they can be left on indefinitely to reduce condensation when the boat isn't in use.

The installation of a shore supply system

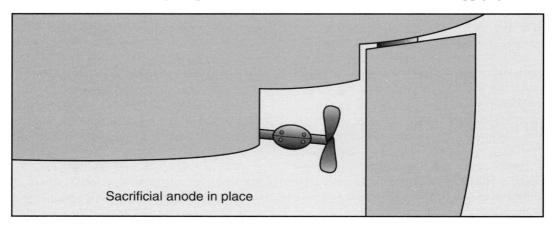

Sacrificial anode in place

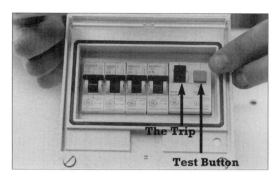

The Trip

Test Button

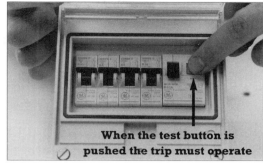

When the test button is pushed the trip must operate

Before using any appliance, check that the circuit breaker (RCCB) is working. Push the test button and the trip must operate. Later, if at any time the current out of the boat doesn't equal the current coming in, the breaker will trip. This may save your life!

needs to be done by a qualified electrician to a professional standard using domestic fittings. It should have its own separate control panel mounted well away from the low voltage supply panel.

The problem of safety with a high voltage system is sometimes dealt with by using a device called an isolating transformer. This ensures that the boat's supply is separated from the mains earth, thus reducing risks of shock and also reducing potential leakage currents which can accelerate electrolytic corrosion.

An alternative, and much better, safety protection system is provided by fitting two circuit breakers. The first serves the same function as those described earlier: it protects the boat against currents in excess of anything the installation is designed to handle, usually about 30 A. In such a system the earth wire must be connected to a boat earth. 'Boat earth' is not the engine block or the sacrificial anode but is a separate plate fitted under water. An alternative to a 'boat earth' is to provide a three-wire ring main for the shore supply and to connect the earth wire to the shore earth, but this is less reliable.

The other circuit breaker is literally a life-saver. It is called a Residual Current Circuit Breaker (RCCB for short) and works in a different way. Its function is to detect small differences in the current flowing between the live line and earth or between the neutral line and earth. If such a difference exists the current flowing into the boat is not the same as that flowing out. Only one explanation of such a situation is possible: some of the input must be leaking to earth. That could be due to insulation breakdown, or faulty equipment, but it could also be due to one of the crew touching a live terminal while being earthed. The RCCB is sensitive to very tiny current differences and will trip out very fast at about 30 milliamps, that is, 0.03 A. It provides excellent safety protection since this is too small a current to kill.

It is normal to have a charging circuit included in the AC mains installation so that the boat batteries can be put on charge as soon as the supply is connected.

The shore link cable

The connection on the pontoon is a special one consisting of a round socket with a cover and it often has a bayonet twist and lock fitting or a screw collar, though some in Europe have spring-loaded covers which grip the cable.

On board there will be a fixed plug into which the boat end of the free cable connects. A plug is used because the live side is on the cable not the panel. Live exposed terminals

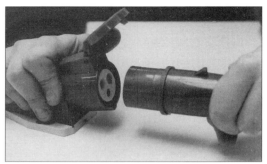
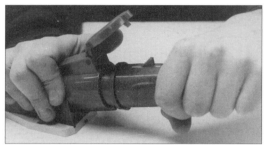
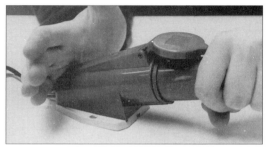

Hook up the boat to the shore supply, using the 3-pin marine-grade plugs and sockets.

aren't a good idea!

The cable linking boat to shore should be at least as long as the boat to reach remote pontoon sockets and is terminated with a standard plug. Be careful to make sure this cable is slack enough, when in use, so it doesn't become a mooring line as the boat moves.

In most marinas you are not permitted to use your own cable and must rent one of their's. You may need an adaptor at the boat-end of the marina supply cable to match their connector into your system.

PORTABLE GENERATORS

Petrol driven portable 240 V AC generators can be useful to supply power tools for maintenance jobs, or for trickle-charging batteries on board during lay-up periods. On a small yacht (less than 11 metres) I don't carry a portable generator with me all the time – it takes up stowage space and also means storing petrol, possibly below decks.

A portable generator.

TREATMENT FOR ELECTRIC SHOCK

Although the average boat has a 12 volt system there are plenty of opportunities to get a high-voltage electric shock. Many marinas offer mains connection facilities, and when working on the boat you may use power tools supplied with 240 volts from the mains or a generator. Some navigational instruments such as radar can produce a high voltage even after being switched off – and you may even be struck by lightning! The treatment given below is appropriate for any of these.

The effects of electric shock are multiple: surface burns where the current enters the body or where it exits to earth, internal injuries, fractures and dislocations due to muscle spasm and, most seriously, an interruption of the rhythm of the heart causing an irregular beat or stopping the heart altogether. There are also temporary effects on the nervous system such as blindness and loss of consciousness.

Treatment

1. Do not approach the casualty if he is still connected to the electric current. Make sure that the current is switched off before you touch him.
2. If the casualty is unconscious check immediately to see if he is breathing and has a pulse. If he is not breathing and/or has no pulse immediately begin the resuscitation procedure. This is explained in detail in a sister publication from Fernhurst Books entitled *First Aid Afloat* by Dr Robert Haworth.
3. If the casualty is breathing and has a pulse but is unconscious put him into the recovery position.
4. If the casualty is conscious get him into a safe, protected place, lie him down and reassure him. Treat for shock by putting rolled-up clothing under his legs to raise them. Keep his head low. Do not encourage him to sit up.
5. Look for burns on the surface and treat them by covering with a clean dressing such as a sterile dressing if the area is small, or with a triangular bandage if the area is large.
6. If he is fully conscious give two paracetamol tablets for the pain.
7. Stay with him and reassure him, checking his response every 10 minutes. If he becomes unconscious place him in the recovery position. If he stops breathing give artificial respiration.
8. Check the casualty to see if he has any other injuries due to muscle contraction at the time of shock. These will be fractures or dislocations – treatment is explained in *First Aid Afloat*.
9. If the casualty has no such injuries, is conscious and has no extensive burns there is no urgency to get him to medical attention once the electric current is switched off.
10. If he has other injuries or extensive burns, you will need to get urgent medical attention. Assess the extent of the burns. Then call the emergency services.

7 Instrumentation & extras

Production boats are seldom fitted with a full range of instruments as standard. You may get an echosounder, a log and possibly a VHF. Manufacturers generally prefer to supply the rest as 'free' extras or as options. In some ways this is good because most of us have our own preferences and it's pointless to fill a new boat with lots of goodies you don't actually want.

POWER REQUIREMENTS

So long as the builder has allowed for additions in calculating the alternator size, has provided some spare circuits, and has made provision for mounting them, you can add what you need later. Even if he hasn't done any of these, it's possible to fit a more powerful alternator to most engines, though with a new boat this is best discussed prior to building. Additional wiring requirements can also be incorporated more easily at this stage.

There is a price to pay for extra electric power: it consumes engine power. A kilowatt of electrical power needs approximately 1.75 horsepower from the engine. This means that a bigger alternator will cost you more in fuel and will give you less available energy at the propeller. If your engine is a small one, say 18 HP, which is not uncommon, a 10% power reduction at the propeller may prove dangerous.

CALCULATION OF DEMAND

Manufacturer's handbooks and catalogues tell you the power consumption of each piece of electronic equipment originally fitted. Make a list of the wattage of everything, both fitted and planned. Do not forget things like pumps, plug-in spotlights and the like. Add all these together, allowing a further 20% for future unplanned additions and divide the answer by the voltage of the supply. Now add the charging current needed for all the batteries together. This total is what your alternator could be called upon to supply.

In practice you are unlikely to have everything switched on at one time, but it makes a good starting point. The maximum output current from the alternator, which is given in its spec, must be at least equal to the average load plus 10% if the batteries are to maintain their charge and everything is going to work as intended. This exercise is particularly valuable if no ammeter is fitted.

Managing resources

If the alternator output is close to the calculated consumption, you will have to manage your resources more carefully. Make sure you charge the batteries regularly and for long enough periods. If one of them gets low, charge it on its own for several hours. Keep lights to a minimum and switch off anything not actually in use. This is good practice in any event.

Avoid running the engine for long periods on the mooring since it does it no good. If you sail you can always motor-sail to windward while charging batteries, and point higher, or use the engine to increase your average speed.

FLUCTUATING AND LOW VOLTAGES

Alternators don't produce a smooth output voltage and modern electronics are sensitive to supply fluctuations. A fully-charged battery in good condition will smooth out minor fluctuations before they reach the control panel. Intermittent troubles, such as things switching themselves off or interfering with each other, may sometimes be an indication of impending battery failure; in fact, of a low or fluctuating voltage problem. In this case, treating the cause rather than the symptom is the best course of action.

Good quality modern equipment is fitted with internal voltage control circuitry which can cope with small fluctuations. Problems usually arise from high current devices, particularly motors which take a high transient current as they start to turn. Surge spikes do most of the damage. These can occur when high current devices are switched on and off, even with batteries in good condition. Electric winches and the anchor windlass are particular culprits. The crank motor (starter) shouldn't give trouble if it has its own battery. However, it is a good idea to turn off all instruments temporarily before starting the engine.

In larger yachts separate regulated supplies are sometimes used for delicate equipment but this is generally impractical in smaller craft.

So long as the problem isn't the battery, it's possible to fit surge suppressors in the input lines to affected items. There are two types of suppressor: one is capacitive and should be fitted across the input terminals of the equipment and the other is inductive and needs to be in series with each line. Both work by recognising the rapidly changing nature of the surge. The capacitive type effectively shorts out the spike before it enters the equipment. The inductive type takes the tops off spikes and can act as a total block to very steep ones. Suppressors do not affect the DC component of the supply.

MOISTURE PROBLEMS

Many of the instruments on a yacht will be fitted below decks and will be subject only to atmospheric moisture. Others, of necessity, have to be fitted in the cockpit or on a bridge over the companionway. These exposed displays suffer most. Good quality display meters designed for the purpose are protected by filling them with gas, usually dry nitrogen at a little above atmospheric pressure. They can also be protected by desiccators (tubes of water-absorbent crystals). Instruments protected in this way seldom give trouble. If they do, professional treatment will be necessary. The first telltale sign of moisture leakage is condensation on the inside of the glass.

At the cheaper end of the scale, where 'O' ring seals or even flat neoprene gaskets have been used, it may be possible to open up the instrument. Remove the desiccator (if fitted). Thoroughly dry any damp. A hairdryer is ideal for this purpose, providing you take care not to overheat the delicate components. The desiccator is a tube or package containing crystals which readily absorb moisture from the air. Often the desiccant changes colour between its active and spent condition. Such devices can be revived in a fairly warm oven (150° C). Alternatively the whole cartridge can be replaced.

Cure the leak by replacing the seals, though sometimes refitting with a silicone sealant coating may suffice.

Look out for any new signs of moisture after refitting. A good time to check is when the air temperature cools in the evening or after a rain shower. Failure to deal with the early signs may result in expensive damage to instruments.

REMOVAL OF AN INSTRUMENT FOR REPAIR

It will often be more convenient and less costly to remove an instrument for repair rather than to call out a service engineer. This should not be too difficult, provided some simple rules are followed.

- Make sure that the instrument, rather than its associated supply or sensors, is at fault.
- Trace the wiring from the instrument back to its distribution panel or sub-panel. (Many display instruments have their own sub-panels. These may be fitted behind panels or in other obscure places. They should be sealed, but sometimes the integrity of the seal has been overridden by a poor cable connection.)
- The head-lining may need to be removed to get at the wiring. Note the method of fitting and orientation before removing such fixings so that they can be replaced correctly. (Small pieces of masking tape can be used to fix the orientation when in doubt. Do the same for the individual wires before removing them from their terminals.)
- Once all wires are disconnected, remove the instrument from the bulkhead. Bulkhead-mounted displays may have

A small submersible centrifugal bilge pump.

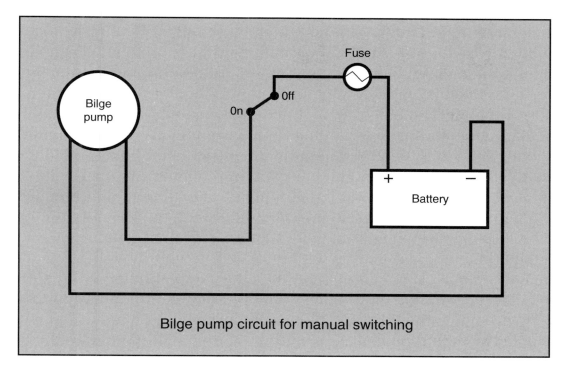

Bilge pump circuit for manual switching

blind plugs to cover screw fittings. These must be removed to get at the screws. They should be punched through and then carefully prised out taking care not to damage the surround. New plugs will be supplied by the instrument's manufacturer on its return from servicing.

- Refit in the reverse order. Don't over-tighten the fixing screws or you may distort the case, damage the seal or even crack the glass. Where the instrument will be exposed to the weather, bed it in mastic to prevent water getting behind it.
- Wire-up and test the item before finishing the refit.

ELECTRIC PUMPS

Bilge pumps

Only fit electric bilge pumps as a back-up: they won't work when they are most needed – when the batteries are under water! Pumps use a lot of energy getting rid of water, as anyone knows who has ever had to use a hand bilge pump in anger.

The most common electric bilge pumps used in sailing yachts are the small submersible centrifugal ones. There is no lift with these, the whole pump being under water. They can usually cope with a head of up to 3 m (that is, the outlet must be no more than 3 m above the pump). These pumps can handle variable flow rates (typically from 800–4000 litres per hour) depending on cost. This is much too slow to deal with a serious leak, but they are useful in getting rid of water from small seepage leaks or from rain water. The standard wiring circuit for such a pump is shown in the diagram.

The leads on submersible pumps are sealed-in. They're seldom long enough to reach the control panel and it's essential, therefore, that the connections to the extension wires are made above the likely bilge water level.

It is common practice to add a float switch

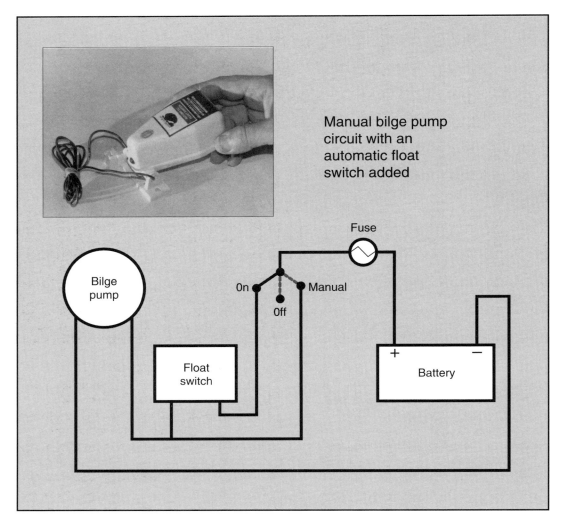

Manual bilge pump circuit with an automatic float switch added

to such a pump so that it will operate automatically when the water level exceeds a set minimum. The additions needed for such a circuit are given in the diagram. Provision must be made to override the float switch as shown in the diagram. Such a system can be wired direct to the battery, and so left on when the boat is unoccupied. Beware, a small leak can drain the battery while the pump drains the bilge. Avoid this by replacing the two-position switch with a three-position one to give an 'Off' position.

Centrifugal pumps run at very high

speeds and are easily stopped by debris dropped in the bilges (particularly matches). A fine-mesh strum box is essential to protect them. If your pump is fitted with a coarse mesh or no mesh at all, use a piece of curtain netting or the foot of a pair of tights to cover the inlet.

The main cause of failure in this type of pump is a breakdown of the shaft seal, allowing water to reach the motor. The commonest cause of seal breakdown is almost impossible to prevent – hair passing through the strum box, however fine the filter.

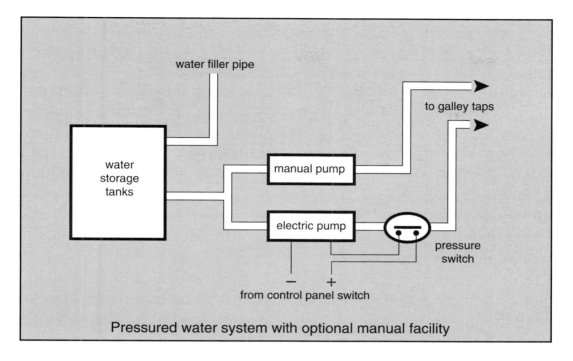

Pressured water system with optional manual facility

The hair wraps round the shaft and cuts into the neoprene seal. The only real solution is to make sure that hair doesn't get dropped into the bilges!

Reciprocating pumps suck from above the bilge level and must be self-priming. They can cope with much larger volumes of water (around 10 000–50 000 litres per hour on small boats) but they take a good deal of current to operate. One that could deal on its own with a serious leak (from a collision, for example) would need so much power as to be impractical on the average 9–12 m sailing yacht. However, provided the engine is running, such a pump can give precious extra time in which to deal with the problem. **Manual pumps should, however, always be fitted in addition to electric ones.**

Fresh water pumps

Older yachts and some smaller modern ones sometimes have mechanical foot or hand pumps to bring fresh water from the tanks to the sink. These are being replaced nowadays by small electrical lift pumps.

The pressures involved are not high and this sort of pump generally gives good reliable service. They work by means of a pressure operated switch. When the tap is turned, 'on' the pressure on one side of a small diaphragm drops, the diaphragm then distorts and this causes the contacts on a micro-switch to close and operate the pump. Any damage to the diaphragm, or water penetration into the switch, can cause the pump to fail. The circuit involved is shown in the diagram.

You may be able to adjust the pressure needed to operate the switch. The adjustment can be made via a small grub-screw, or by simply bending a metal tang. Reset if the pump hunts (comes on in short bursts) when the taps are all off, but first make sure the tank is full or the hunting may be caused by bubbles in the pump feed! The pump may also be affected by a dirty, or old, in-line purifying filter causing unwanted back pressure.

If you make passages away from shore it's wise to have an alternative method of taking water from the fresh water tank. The simplest method is to tee in a mechanical foot-operated pump, via a changeover valve (as shown in the diagram), into the feed pipe from the tank and to feed the outlet from that pump directly to a separate cold water outlet at the galley. This effectively means that either the mechanical pump or the electric one can be used at any time. The mechanical pump feed must be connected to the tank side of the electric pump so that the pressure switch is not affected.

In this case, if the electric pump fails, you only need to flip the control valve and use the mechanical pump.

Showers are frequently supplied from one, common, fresh water pump. If the shower won't work when the galley supply is still doing its job, look for an independent pump supplying it.

All the electric pumps are often wired to a common circuit on the control panel. So one faulty pump can cut them all off. The commonest culprit in such cases is the shower drain pump, since it is usually least used and can seize up.

8 The electrical toolkit

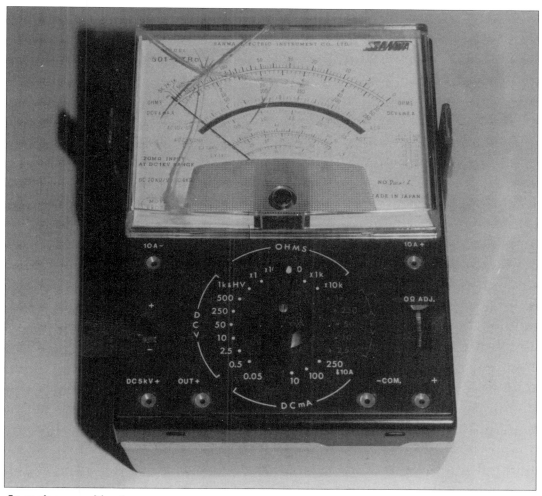

An analogue multimeter.

The standard boat toolkit will contain most of the tools needed for electrical work, but a few extras will make electrical faults much easier to find and deal with.

You'll need screwdrivers to fit the small, cross-head screws used in most electrical equipment. Buy a pair of wire strippers, a pair of pointed-nosed pliers and a pair of electrician's pliers and spanners to fit 3 mm to 10 mm nuts. A pair of tweezers are useful or, better still, if you have a doctor friend, a pair of locking forceps. A 12 V soldering iron plus

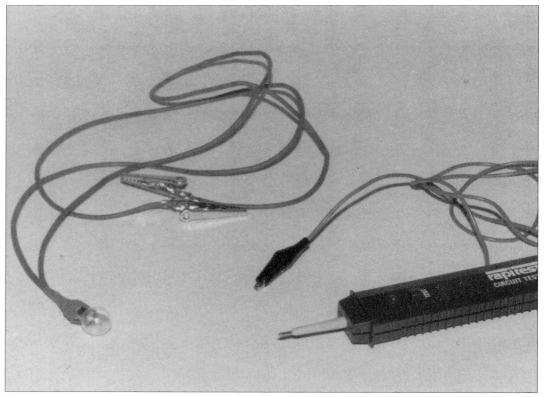

Circuit testers, for live 12 V circuits (left) and non-live circuits (right) (this tester has an integral battery).

multi-core solder, a hydrometer, a small multimeter and a continuity tester complete the essentials.

If you want to go to town you could add a heavy, gas heated, soldering iron and a crimping tool plus a selection of crimps.

The analogue multimeter should preferably have one of its voltage ranges with 15 V full scale, though they are sometimes hard to find. A current range up to 10 A is useful and it should have at least one resistance range. A simple and effective continuity tester can be purchased for a

pound or so at most motor factors. This is used for checking non-live circuits.

The neon tester screwdrivers used for testing live domestic wiring will not, unfortunately, work at low voltages. To test live circuits use the multimeter or, for only a few pence, make yourself a tester using a low wattage bulb on a pair of wires each about 30 cm long and terminated with small crocodile clips. This is often easier to use in confined spaces. It is particularly useful when all you need is to find out if electricity is getting through to a particular point.

ELECTRICAL SPARES

Tools will be useless unless you have replacements parts for potentially faulty items. Use a separate plastic toolbox for electrical spares.

It should contain:

- replacement bulbs for all navigation and domestic light fittings
- a selection of fuses and a spare circuit-breaker
- tubes of silicone grease and sealant
- wire in several sizes
- a couple of rolls of insulating tape in two colours
- a roll of self-amalgamating tape
- a strip of connecting block
- a spare deck gland
- a few cable ties
- replacements for special plugs especially for the VHF, Decca/Loran and GPS. (The small ones with a bayonet-type locking collar are called 'BNC' and the larger ones with a screw locking ring are 'Amphenol' connectors.)

Equipped with all the items listed you can deal with most electrical problems.

9 Preventative maintenance & testing

Many electrical faults can be anticipated and even dealt with before they appear as problems. Check the components listed in the following table before they cause total failure or serious damage.

SYSTEMATIC FAULT-FINDING

Fault-finding must be systematic and logical. Faults that occur at sea are potentially life-threatening. Realising this often leads to panic, making the job very much harder.

I once took a yacht in tow which had become becalmed in fog and was drifting onto rocks. The yacht had a petrol engine. The crew had been trying to start it for two hours. Fifteen minutes after we started the tow, the skipper called across to say that he had solved the problem: the distributor had been full of condensation. This should have been easy to find, but fear, and perhaps lack of forethought, had prevented a systematic approach.

Always start by identifying all the symptoms. Frequently, the obvious symptom is not the only one and a secondary indicator may give a more useful clue to the real problem. At home you would first check that the power is on and that the fuse hasn't blown. The same very basic approach applies on any boat.

STRATEGY FOR FINDING A FAULT IN A CIRCUIT

If a fuse or circuit breaker has failed, you must find out why. Try to make a physical examination looking for signs of burning, chafe or a loose connection that may have produced a short. Use a continuity tester to see if either terminal has a path to earth or to an adjoining wire. Before the fuse is replaced or the CBE reset it is essential to get to the bottom of the cause of the failure. Remember that the device was fitted for protection and it did its job!

EQUIPMENT FAULTS

If any item of equipment fails to provide the expected output, check that it's getting a proper supply (what is the voltage across its input terminals?), check the connections to and from it (are they tight and undamaged?), check its controls (are they set correctly?).

Where you can't identify the fault, you may need to look for ways round the problem. You will need to ask yourself a series of questions, starting with: Can we do without this? Do we have a spare? Can we use something else instead?

If the answer to all three of these really is, 'no', you may need to anchor, heave to, change course or even ask for outside help. The point is that any such decision must be arrived at rationally.

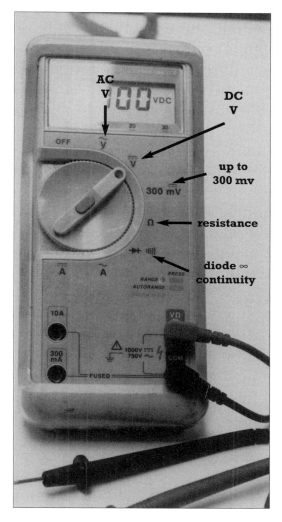

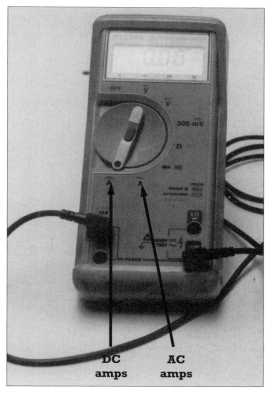

A basic multimeter showing some of its ranges. Note the separate terminals used for high currents.

JUNCTION BOXES & TERMINAL BLOCKS

Always remove the cover when checking a junction box to see if moisture has got in and caused damage. This is particularly so in waterproof boxes, once they have aged a little. Most are fitted with neoprene grommets and seals: it's always worth checking them for signs of degradation. Smear a small amount of silicone grease on an 'O' ring or seal before refitting the cover.

Terminal blocks should only be used in situations where they are unlikely to be affected by drips or immersion. Always make a drip-loop when wiring mast cables to a block below the deck. Otherwise any water finding its way through the deck gland will reach the terminals and won't only destroy the connections but will be able to wick back up the cable. Wicking can go a long way and will probably mean replacing the entire cable.

USING A MULTIMETER
(analogue or digital (DMM))

Your multimeter can be used to measure voltage, current or resistance. An analogue meter is best for indicating trends, a digital meter (as in the photos on pages 75, 78 & 79) is best for sensitivity. Modern DMMs have both digital and analogue scales.

1. Voltage measurements

Set the meter to the voltage range that covers your boat's system (if it's a 12 V system, select the 15 V range). To test for voltage, switch on the circuit. Then carefully connect the probes across (i.e., in parallel with) the item you're testing. For example, connect the tester across the battery terminals to test the supply voltage, or across the terminals of a lamp to check it's getting a supply. When doing this, connect the meter's (+ve) terminal to the positive side of the supply, then the (–ve) to the negative supply. Take care that your connections aren't causing a short circuit – i.e., a bridge for electricity to flow where it shouldn't. If in any doubt, switch off the circuit while you set up your meter's probes.

Most multimeters are supplied with alternative clip and probe terminals to help you test for voltage around a live circuit. To do this, fit a clip to the meter's negative terminal, and a probe to the meter's positive terminal. Put the clip onto the negative of the circuit, then move the probe about the circuit to check voltages, again taking care not to short-circuit the battery.

2. Current measurements

You won't often need to measure current but occasionally it's useful. To measure current, the meter must be inserted into the circuit in series. This means you will have to disconnect something and bridge the gap with the meter.

Before starting the process, select the highest current range available on your meter. The easiest place to break the circuit is at a fuse-holder or switch. Don't test for current however, if a fuse has blown or a switch tripped.
Find the fault first!
To check the current in a working circuit proceed as follows:
1. Select the highest current range on the meter.
2. Turn off the supply.
3. Remove the fuse, or, if going across a switch, make sure it is in the 'off' position.
4. Use clips on the leads to connect across the fuse-holder or switch.
5. Check for possible short circuits from your connections.
6. Turn on the supply.
7. With an analogue meter, if the meter needle goes backwards turn off the supply and reverse the connections. A DMM will indicate + or - flow.
8. If the reading on an analogue meter is very small, you can then adjust the meter range switch one step at a time until you get a clear needle deflection. Modern DMMs have auto-range selection.
9. Read the current and then switch off the supply before reconnecting the circuit.

Batteries can supply very high currents. Never connect the current meter directly across the supply since this will almost certainly destroy it!

3. Resistance measurements

The multimeter can be used to measure the resistance of a single component, or of a section of wire. This is very useful in fault finding.

The meter measures resistance by passing a current from its internal battery through the item to be tested – i.e., what's between its probes.

1. First, select the ohm scale.
2. Zero the meter by touching the probes together. There is consequently no resistance between them. Now adjust the meter until it reads zero.
3. Switch off the circuit. Put the probes across the item of interest and read off its resistance. A high resistance may mean the component is dead, or a joint is 'dry', or the wires between the probes are broken. You can test fuses, bulbs and switches too. Many DMMs have buzzer circuits to do this.

Places to use resistance measuring

You can use resistance measurement if you suspect a short-circuit to the mast or to a metal pulpit or even to an adjoining circuit.

1. Disconnect the suspect circuit from its supply on both sides.
2. Connect one lead from the meter to the suspect circuit using a clip connector.
3. With a probe fitted on the other lead touch the suspect item (mast, wiring, etc.).
4. The needle should not move (analogue). A digital readout should indicate maximum resistance (max MΩ). (You are measuring the resistance of the contact between the mast and the circuit. This should be high – i.e. no contact between them.)
5. In damp conditions a very small movement is just acceptable but probably implies only that attention will be needed soon.
6. Anything more than a slight movement means a partial short circuit.
7. To fine down the exact location, disconnect parts of the suspect circuit in turn until you have isolated the offending section.
8. This wire or component can then be replaced or repaired.

Note: The multimeter is not the best way to check for leakage since it will only be checking at 1.5 V or less. A wire, or a component, may appear satisfactory at this voltage but may leak at higher voltages. A special instrument is needed to find such faults but this is too expensive an item for the general handyman.

To check voltage

1.1 To check voltage (e.g. of a battery). Select DC Volts. Put the red probe on the +ve terminal and the black probe on the –ve. This battery is flat.

To check current

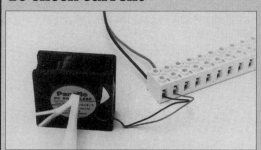

2.1 To check current e.g., through this little fan (we've stuck some paper streamers onto it to show it's working).

To find a break in a fuse or a wire

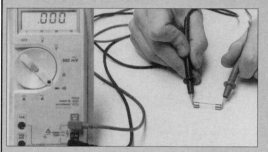

3.1 To check resistance, select ohms (Ω). Attach a probe to each side of the fuse. Resistance is zero – the fuse is OK.

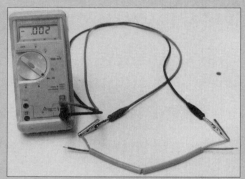

3.2 Again, is this wire broken? Follow the same technique. Resistance is minimal – no break.

To check the continuity of an alternator stator

4.1 Again select the ohms scale (Ω). The multimeter's battery attempts to pass a current round the circuit and so measures resistance between the probes.

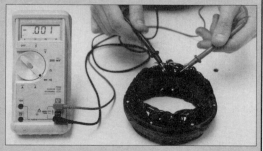

4.2 Resistance is virtually zero – this alternator stator is fine.

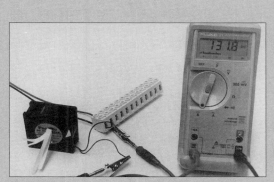

2.2 Select mA on the multimeter and connect it in series with the fan.

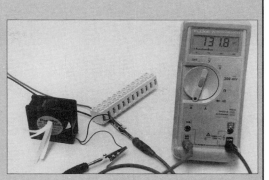

2.3 The multimeter reads 131 mA. The fan appears to running fine.

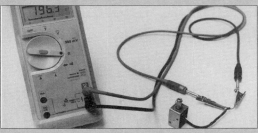

3.3 To measure resistance the multimeter passes a current around a circuit, in this case a solenoid, and measures the resistance found in the circuit. Here it is high at 196 Ω – the circuit is broken.

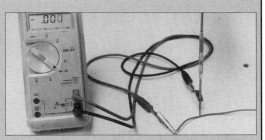

3.4 To find exactly where a wire is broken inside its insulation, first connect one probe to the end of the wire. Then, move a spiked probe along the wire until the resistance increases – you will then have passed the break.

To check for a leak to earth

5.1 Here a cable has chafed against a metal plate. Select ohms (Ω). Connect one probe to the plate and the other to the wire. They form a circuit. The meter reads 4.1 Ω. There is a leak to earth.

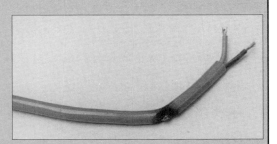

5.2 Here's the chafed wire that caused the problem.

MAKING A DRIP-LOOP IN A WIRE

Water collects on exposed cables. Though a cable's insulation prevents the penetration of water to its conductors, it will wick along the insulation to the terminals unless you use drip-loops.

To form a drip-loop allow for extra length when cutting a new cable. At the higher end, where the cable enters a mast fitting make a loop in the wire such that any water collecting on it will have to run uphill to enter the fitting or the mast. At the bottom, where the cable passes through the deck, use a cable gland. Cable glands have adjustable collars that can be tightened onto a cable, stopping water getting past. Despite the cable gland it's still a good idea to include a drip-loop below the gland below the deck. This'll protect the cable–terminal joint should any water get past the gland. The loop need not be big, 2 or 3 cm radius is quite enough. The simplest way to make one is to tape the cable back up to the underside of the deck once it has come through the gland, before making the connection.

DECK SOCKETS & GLANDS

Deck sockets and plugs are suitable only for temporary connections – to such things as inspection lamps and rigging-hung anchor lights. All permanent wiring should use deck glands. Only one cable should pass through each gland. Where bunches of wires are installed together leaks are inevitable unless they are well bedded-in with mastic. The neoprene seal must be loosened completely while a new cable is being drawn through it. A little silicone grease wiped onto the wire will lubricate the entry and prevent wear to the seal. Draw the cable through the gland slowly because considerable heat can be generated by the friction caused between the cable and seal which may be enough to soften or melt it.

Whenever a seal shows signs of wear, distortion or degradation, replace it. Sealing compound can be used as a temporary expedient but will never provide a long term repair once the original has failed.

Treading on a deck gland can damage both the wire and the seal. Where risk of this is high (at the foot of the mast for example) construct a box with a sloping, hinged cover. Deck sockets tend to have a short life unless they are serviced regularly. Ensure that the screw covers are tight and that the seals are free from damage and lightly greased. Spray the connections with WD40, 'Electrolube', or similar product, to protect them. The plugs on appliances used in such sockets also need attention, especially when they are only used infrequently.

REPLACING WIRES IN THE MAST

Wires in the mast need replacing far more often than actually happens, because the job appears tricky. This isn't helped if the boatbuilder didn't fit drawcords, or if the ducts are too narrow.

There are ways to get round the problem. If you don't mind heights it is easier to do the job with the mast standing. In any event it will

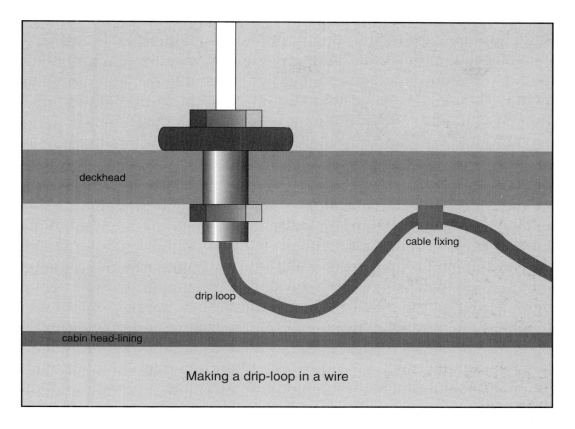

deckhead

cable fixing

drip loop

cabin head-lining

Making a drip-loop in a wire

always be easier to deal with a potential defect in harbour before it becomes a real problem at sea.

How to do it

Use twin or three-core cable for mast electrics. The extra sheathing gives better protection and it is much easier to pull a multicored cable through. To replace existing wires start by checking to see if a drawcord is fitted. If it is, attach the new wire to the bottom end of the cord very securely. Use a rolling hitch, then cover the knot with several layers of insulating tape. Pull the join tight to test it and join the end of the wire to the cord with more tape. This helps prevent snags and makes pulling the cable through much easier.

If no cord is fitted you can use the wire you're replacing as a drawcord and at the same time fit a new cord for future use. Begin

by joining the new cable firmly to the old. Now attach a length of thin (2 mm) cordage to the join and tape it over. Carefully pull the old wire out dragging the new one after it. The cord you pulled through with new cable is now a drawcord available for use next time.

To add an extra wire when no drawcord is fitted you can still use an existing wire as a starter cord. Attach the new drawcord, together with the new wire, to one of the existing wires and pull the old wire through, drawing the new wire and cord into place as before. Now disconnect the new wire from the join, temporarily secure it and attach a second drawcord. Pulling the first cord back through now puts the old wire back in place and leaves the second drawcord for future use.

Pulling new wires through a standing mast is easier to achieve by taking them up from

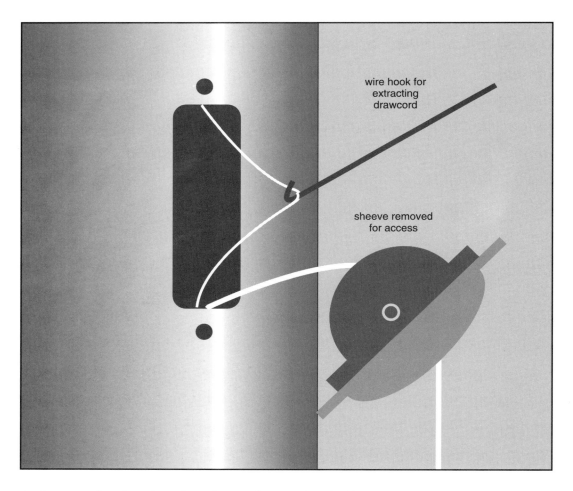

wire hook for
extracting
drawcord

sheeve removed
for access

the bottom rather than down from the top. So always make the join at the bottom. Wrap tape over the joint to make it smooth. If a line becomes difficult to pull don't force it. Instead lower it a little, then try again. Most snags result from the join catching on a bolt or pop-rivet end inside the mast. Gravity will help free the snag if you are pulling from the top. Once everything is in place pull the drawcord tight and tie it firmly in place at both the top and bottom of the mast so that it stays there and doesn't chafe.

Adding mast items part way up

To fit an extra deck light, or some other electrical item, part way down the mast you may need to use the existing full mast drawcord. Attach the new cable to the drawcord at the bottom of the mast as before, but also include an extra length of new cord tied to the old one. This is for recovering the old drawcord. Prepare a hook from a piece of stiff wire which will pass through the hole in the mast and which will also go easily round the cord.

If there is no convenient entry point, drill the cable entry hole oversize by 4 mm, then clean it to remove any sharp edges.

Using the hook and a pencil torch for light, catch hold of the draw cord within the mast (it helps if you have an assistant). The cord will

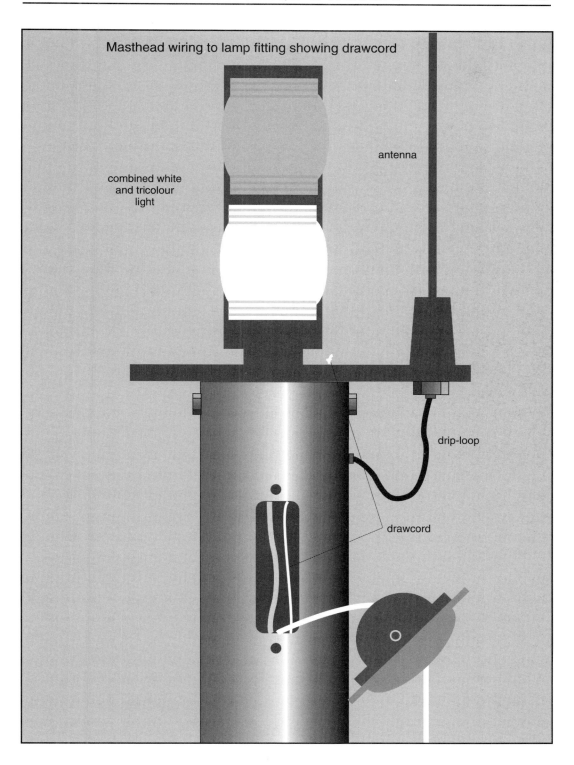

Masthead wiring to lamp fitting showing drawcord

combined white and tricolour light

antenna

drip-loop

drawcord

need to be fairly tight so that you can hook it. You may need to free the halyards and shake them about until you can see the cord. Next slacken the lower end, draw a loop of it through the hole and pull it up until the cable end passes through the hole. Detach the cable and tie a knot in it about 30 cm from the end, to stop it slipping back.

The extra cord can now be tied to the original and pulled back from the bottom, where the original draw cord can be re-secured.

Fit a grommet over the cable to protect it where it enters the mast. Self-amalgamating tape can be used to replace a grommet if necessary but this really is only a second-best choice. Leave a drip-loop of about 10–15 cm to prevent water running down the wire before completing the fitting.

MASTHEAD CONNECTIONS IN GENERAL

Most antennae have the coaxial cable moulded to them. This virtually precludes moisture problems but it also means that replacing the cable generally involves replacing the whole antenna.

Other masthead connections are less protected. Light fittings often have breathing holes at the bottom of the fitting to allow moisture to evaporate. This approach seems to be more effective than trying to seal a device which is subject to such large temperature variations. When the lamp is on the heat generated will dry the fitting in a few hours. On boats where the lights are seldom used, make regular checks of both socket and bulb contacts and use WD40 or Electro-lube on the connections. Don't forget to polish the lens!

Wind instrument sensors have plug-in connectors with screw collars to provide mechanical strength and to prevent water entry. It is best to remove the collar once or twice a season and check the condition of the

'O' ring seal. Replace it if in doubt. Before reconnecting smear the threads lightly with waterproof grease to prevent corrosion. If a collar is allowed to seize up, it will often break during attempts to free it. Replacement of the entire unit is then the only solution. Penetrating oil and a lot of patience may be needed on a neglected fitting to save well over a hundred pounds.

CONNECTIONS TO ANTENNAE

Coaxial antennae cables should be directly connected to the plug at the VHF or instrument without any other joins if possible. Unstepping the mast is more difficult using this method but the extra trouble involved is worth it in terms of the resulting reliability.

Coaxial cables are more complex than they may seem. They handle VHF (very high frequency) signals at very low power levels. In such situations, resistance is not so important as 'impedance'. This is the high frequency equivalent of resistance. Use a cable of the correct impedance and keep it in good condition. Both moisture and corrosion can seriously affect coaxial cable, producing losses so great that the effective range of a VHF radio, on transmit, may be cut by as much as 90%. An instrument called a reflectometer can be used to check this easily. Your local service engineer should be able to do this for you at least once each season.

The VHF is not the only RF (radio frequency) device on board. Decca/Loran, GPS, even the echosounder, all use coaxial cables. With the echosounder not only the cable's condition, but also its length, is critical. The cable supplied with the hull sensor should never be cut. Degradation of this cable is indicated by the need for increased gain to get a reasonable signal. It is best to replace the transducer completely in such cases. Repair is well beyond any DIY capability – nor is it cost-effective.

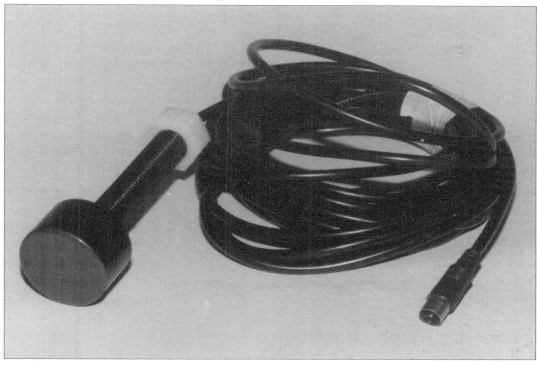

An echosounder transducer.

THROUGH-DECK WIRING

All other wires above deck should pass through the deck via proper deck glands. Mast wires can be connected to a junction box or terminal block above the head lining after passing through these glands. A separate gland is needed for each cable. On older boats, you may find deck plugs used for permanent through-deck connections. consider replacing these with glands as soon as they show signs of degradation. Deck glands are not only cheaper; they are also easier to fit, more reliable and have a longer life.

REWIRING PULPIT OR PUSHPIT LIGHTS

The most difficult wire to replace on a boat is the one supplying a light on the pushpit or pulpit. The original wire is often run through the pipework and probably has no drawcord.

It's frequently a tight fit at both the entry and the exit holes.

A wire passed up through the open end of the pipe is generally easier to pull through from above since the entry is not restricted. As it's completely hidden, it also makes for a neater, safer job. More dismantling may be needed however, and you'll need two people for the job, but if you can gain access it's well worth the effort.

Always use twin-sheathed cable. Even if you're using a junction box below the deck, don't cut the new cable until you've finished the installation above deck – instead just unwind it from the reel as required. If you have to use a short length tie a knot about 250 mm from the free end to avoid the risk of pulling it all right through. Temporarily solder or firmly twist the new wire pair onto the old, making sure the joint is good before starting to pull (you may need to pull quite

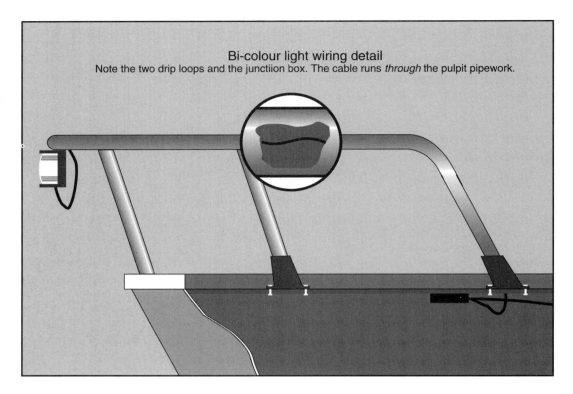

Bi-colour light wiring detail
Note the two drip loops and the junctiion box. The cable runs *through* the pulpit pipework.

hard). Wrap the join with insulating tape until it is the same size as the outer sheath. This makes it stronger and also easier to feed through. If the wire passes through a deck gland before going into the pipe, push the new wire up through it before making the join.

Disconnect the old wires at the lamp and pull the cable end out of the lamp housing. With one person feeding the new cable into the pipe, and the other pulling at the old one, it should be possible to work the replacement through. Leave any existing grommets in the pipe if they are in good condition and not too tight a fit on the wire. You won't be able to fit new ones unless you first fit a drawcord. Use washing-up liquid to lubricate the old grommets. Pull sufficient cable through to the light fitting to make a large drip-loop. This spare does not just provide a drip-loop; it also allows the wire to be re-terminated at a later date if necessary. Tie a

knot in the cable where it emerges from the pipe and pull any surplus back below decks. Wrap a couple of layers of self-amalgamating tape round the wire to protect it where it goes into the pipe if you have had to leave out the grommets.

Once the new cable is in place you can then feed the end through the lamp housing and connect it.

Should the old wire be broken or jammed in position inside the tubing, you may need to attach the replacement to the outside of the pipework (it's rarely possible to feed a new wire into complex pipework without a draw wire or cord). Cable straps are longer-lasting than tape but the addition of tape, or even a length of plastic hose taped to the pipe at the lower end, helps to protect the cable from abrasion.

Finish the job using a junction box below decks to join the new wires to the old. The bare wires must be clean and bright at the

Fluorescent lighting gives five times as much light per watt as an incandescent bulb.

connections. It may be necessary to replace a cable right back to the control panel if it isn't in good condition but a junction box below deck level usually avoids this.

Junction boxes and blocks must always be marine grade with solid brass terminals. Cadmium or brass-plated steel, often used in domestic circuits, is not good enough in a moist, salty environment and will soon fail. Sadly some builders of production boats still use such terminals. Cadmium-plated brass crimp terminals reduce corrosion risks still further.

Use wire of the correct size for all new and replacement fittings, particularly for long wire runs. The longest run you are going to find on a boat is usually up the mast. The length of the circuit will be the height of the mast plus the distance from the control panel to the foot of mast, times two. There are legal requirements for visibility ranges of all navigation lights. These govern the wattage

rating of bulbs to be used and are laid down in the IRPCS. Voltage losses resulting from using the wrong wire may reduce the brightness below these limits, even with the correct bulb fitted. Quite apart from the law, the primary purpose of navigation lights is to be seen from as far away as possible, so do not scrimp. (Refer to the tables in Chapter 5 for correct wire sizes.)

Inside the mast I prefer the greater protection of twin- or triple-sheathed wires. Boat wire should always be multi-stranded to avoid vibration-generated fatigue failure. Round, rather than flat, outer sheaths on cables make for a better seal in grommets and deck glands.

LOOMS AND ROUTING

If you are replacing a wire try to run it in the same loom, or duct, as the original. Spiral-wrap is good for keeping wiring tight and reducing movement: cable ties or insulating tape are a cheaper alternative. Only use *electrical* insulating tape since some adhesives can affect the cable insulation. If spiral-wrapped bundles of wires (called looms) are run through ducting it will be next to impossible to replace a wire in the loom: without a drawcord fitted you may need to withdraw the entire loom just to run an additional wire. An alternative, and one probably used by the original electrician when installing the loom, is to use a mouse.

An electrician's mouse is a thin, flat, hard-steel strip, often with a spring tip into which is fitted a ball or small wheel. This device can be pushed easily through an empty duct and rather less easily through a crowded one. It is preferable to withdrawing the whole loom. The new wire will of course be free to rattle about once inside, but if twin cable is used the extra sheath layer will protect it.

ADDING EXTRA LIGHTING

Internal cabin lights can increase the battery drain to a surprising degree. Many boatbuilders favour individual bunk spotlights and may add two or three deck-head mounted, general-purpose lights in the saloon. Such fittings frequently take 10 W torpedo shaped bulbs in pairs with the facility to switch on either one or both bulbs.

The total light output from such fittings is often disappointing, even with several on together. So it's common to have most if not all of them on at once. Four bunk spots, three deck-head lights, plus a galley light, a couple in each cabin and one in the heads, together with a 20 W anchor light gives a total approaching 200 W, drawing almost 17 A. One 90 AH battery would, in peak condition, provide about 5 hours use at this rate before failing.

The answer may be to fit fluorescent lighting in the saloon. Fluorescent tubes give out about five times as much light, watt for watt, as an incandescent bulb. The few

problems they introduce can be overcome.

The fittings cost about the same in either case but tubes are a good deal more costly than bulbs (but I have known them to last ten years without replacement). All fluorescent lights, particularly low voltage ones, generate interference. Some of this is radiated and will affect your FM and AM radio receiver – the ones you use for weather forecasts and entertainment. But most interference is carried by the wires. The interference tends to increase with low battery output and can itself be a sign of problems to come. Suppressors, fitted to the lamps, will remove or reduce this type of interference to acceptable proportions. Swapping tubes from fitting to fitting can sometimes stop the trouble since the radiated interference is generated between the trigger circuit and the tube.

Install one or two fluorescent fittings for use when sitting around in harbour, with incandescent lamps retained for use at sea when bright light isn't wanted. It's then no great problem to turn off an offending lamp when you want to catch the forecast or to listen to the radio.

OPTIONS FOR NAVIGATION LIGHTS

In 1988, the IRPCS were changed to allow the use of an all-round masthead white light as an alternative to separate steaming and stern lights on vessels under 20 metres. On vessels built before that date, and on some just after it, this option isn't provided. The arrangement is actually preferred on safety grounds since it makes small craft more visible to large vessels.

It's not difficult to alter the wiring on your boat to provide this facility. The problem is that the stern white and bow bicolour navigation lights are usually commonly wired. All you need is an extra switch in the line to the stern light, so you can switch this off when the masthead white is on. If no masthead all-round white is provided for

TABLE OF FAULTS AND TREATMENT

Component	Fault	Treatment
Battery case and top	dirt deposits attracting moisture	clean and dry
	leaking	professional repair or replace battery
Battery container	damaged	repair or replace
Battery restraints	loose or damaged	tighten or replace
Battery terminal	looseness of connector	clean and tighten
	corrosion	clean, lubricate
	post moves	professional repair needed
Cable joint	broken or damaged	repair or replace
Circuit breakers	corrosion, discolouration	clean
	trips at low load	replace
	physical damage	replace
Deck gland/socket	damp inside	check seal, repair or replace
	damaged	replace
Deck light fitting	loose connection	clean and tighten plus WD40
	damaged lens or housing	replace
	wire end corrosion	strip back and re-terminate
	water in cable	replace cable
Fuse and/or holders	corrosion or cracked glass	replace
	loose	tighten
Interior light fitting	loose bulb	free off springs or replace item
	loose connections	tighten or remake
	movement of parts	adjust or replace fitting
	striplight fails to trigger	clean all contacts – replace tube/starter
Junction box	moisture entry	seal or replace
	corrosion	clean or replace & reseal
	rust signs	replace
Terminal block	loose or broken wires	re-terminate
	loose screws	tighten
	rust	replace with brass fitting
	cracks or brittleness	replace

anchoring you'll need to replace the tricolour with a combined tricolour and all-round white fitting. You'll also need to provide a mast feed for the extra bulb. A three-core cable will do the job since the negative wire may be common to both lights as they'll never be used together. The all-round white can then be used as an anchor light or as a combined steaming and stern light.

Check before you use an existing white masthead light for navigation. The wattage of the bulb may not be sufficient to comply with the IRPCS. Increasing its value may mean having to replace its supply wire. If it becomes necessary to replace the mast cable refer to the wiring size tables in Chapter 5.

10 High current appliances & equipment

REFRIGERATORS

An electric refrigerator is driven by a compressor. During the cooling cycle it may draw around 12 A. A refrigerator is best run from a separate battery unless it is wired through an automatic trip switch which operates at low battery voltage. This is because a refrigerator will warm up when it gets too little power. The thermostat will sense this and demand more power. A refrigerator compressor connected to a low battery will thus come on and either stay on or hunt, quickly flattening what charge is left in the battery. Try using a gas refrigerator instead – it won't draw quite so much current!

POWERED ANCHOR WINCH OR WINDLASS

This is probably the most power-hungry item on any boat. Even a small one may draw anything from 10 A to 40 A from a 12 V battery. This load may be too much for a small sailing vessel, even with the engine running, and a mechanical winch (or a strong back!) may be a wiser choice. On power vessels the alternator will generally have a greater output and high, short-term consumption isn't so important.

The high load in any case means high current, with its associated thick wires. The runs for these will of necessity be long since the alternator is aft and the anchor forward. Any significant voltage drop will cause overheating in addition to the loss of lift

power. The motor is likely to be mounted in the chain locker where it's subject to high moisture levels and is at mechanical risk from the chain. A high standard of wiring and upkeep will be required if the winch (or windlass) is to be reliable.

Thick cable lengths can be reduced by fitting a dedicated battery forward and trickle charging it. Such a system brings its own problems: extra weight forward and ventilation – salt water finding its way into the battery can release toxic fumes in what is usually a sleeping area.

AUTOPILOT

The current requirements of an autopilot are deceptive. While the average power needs may be low it is not uncommon for some of the larger units to draw a current of 10 A, or so, when actuated. Most have a switched motor to provide the power and this will take a high transient starting current. Fuses or circuit breakers as well as the associated wiring will need to be able to cope with these transient loads.

The servo-motor may have its own circuitry with only the control circuits being run from the distribution panel. In such cases the motor wiring must have its own protection and often has a separate supply switch.

Proper adjustment of the sail trim and controls is essential when the unit is in use to avoid excessive battery drain. Given this proviso, an autopilot can be one of the most useful additions you can make to any boat.

HEATERS

Few small boat heaters are electrically driven: gas or diesel is more efficient and makes fewer demands on the electrical system. They mostly work by circulating warm air, using a fan. The continuous consumption is about 1 A to 2 A on a 12 V system. Ignition however is achieved by a glow plug which may take up to 8 A for a short period.

The Eberspacher system, frequently fitted in small boats, is very reliable. It has a number of safety devices included, the most important of which is a thermal cut-out designed to trip if the circulating fan stops (to prevent overheating). Since this device is thermo-electrically operated it is important to allow the system to cool down before breaking the battery supply after switching off. The trip is a common source of problems. To reactivate it, find the mechanical override fitted on the lower surface of the main unit.

HORNS

Electric foghorns are common on power-boats but are seldom fitted on yachts. Anything less than 150 W of audio-power is of little practical use as a signal to a ship's bridge. This requires about 15 A of current on a 12 V system. Most efficient for this job are air horns driven from a small electric powered compressor. They have the added advantage that the electrics can be installed below decks where they are less vulnerable.

11 Devices powered by primary & NiCad cells

Primary cells are used on boats in various small electrical devices from torches to echosounders. All electrolytes are corrosive. It's wise to use the long-life, steel-cased kind of cells which are less likely to corrode. Even button-type miniature cells can leak and cause damage to terminals.

At the end of the season, or when the boat is out of use for a while, remove the cells from the equipment. Store spare dry cells on board in their blister packs: loose batteries kept in a drawer or box may short out and self-discharge. They can even produce sufficient heat to start a fire.

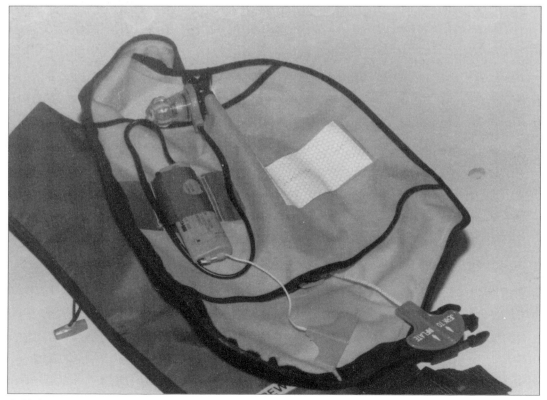

A lifejacket fitted with a seawater-activated safety light.

NiCads, as they are commonly called, shouldn't be used for safety equipment or torches since they give no warning of failure. They are useful in portable radios and are sometimes used as back-up batteries to preserve data in memory-driven devices. (Examples are Decca/Loran and GPS.)

DATA PROTECTION CELLS

These are cells in use only when the equipment is switched off and will often keep the data safe for anything from six months to several years; useful when the boat is laid up. If in doubt, or when the boat is laid up for prolonged periods, take on board a charged service battery every three months and connect it up to the system. The instrument's internal batteries will then be recharged in a few hours. NiCad cells can be recharged rapidly without damage.

SAFETY LIGHTS

Lifejacket lights are usually fitted either with once-only salt water activated cells, or with long-life mercury cells. The latter have a test button which should be used every few months.

Danbuoys and lifebelts may have strobe lights, flashers or even fixed lights of low wattage. The switches for these are often activated by inversion. They must be mounted and stored with the lamp pointing down and should be tested weekly. The switches may be operated by liquid mercury using the battery weight in conjunction with a weak spring. The latter sometimes stick and can need a light tap to activate them. In practice this isn't serious problem since in use they'll hit the water from several metres up.

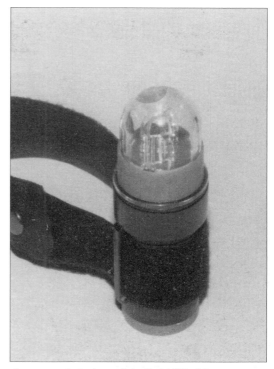

A personal strobe safety-light fitted to an armband.

TORCHES AND LANTERNS

Every boat should be equipped with at least three torches, one low-powered for reading the instruments or checking sail trim without damaging night vision. In addition, pack a set of emergency navigation lights powered by dry cells. A small battery-powered strobe light is a useful safety aid since it can be used to indicate the need for help in the event of total electrical failure. It could also be used as back up in the liferaft and as a personal aid. These lights will flash for about sixteen hours when powered by a single torch cell.

ELECTRICAL FAULT INDICATORS & WHAT THEY MEAN

Symptom	Fault	Checks to confirm
On switching on ignition:		
Ignition light stays off	bulb	use continuity tester
	flat battery	try starting
	switch fault	switch operation
	wiring	continuity/voltage test
Oil warning light stays off	bulb	use continuity tester
	sensor	short sensor terminal to engine
	wiring	continuity tester
Warning alarm sounds	none (test state)	it should stop when engine fires
On switching to 'start':		
Engine fails to turn	flat battery	off-load voltage test (< 12.5 V)
	solenoid	hand operate or override
	starter motor	terminal voltage
	stuck bendix	turn starter by hand
		a smart tap with a hammer
		or spanner may free it
After engine fires:		
Signal alarm stays 'on'	oil pressure	is the lamp on?
	charging	is the ignition lamp on?
	alarm short	wiring shorts
Ignition light stays 'on'	revs too low	increase revs
	alternator wiring	stop engine & run continuity test
	alternator output	voltage test at battery (> 13 V)

Symptom	Fault	Checks to confirm
Oil light stays 'on'	oil level low	dip stick (engine off)
	oil pump fault	oil level correct
		no oil at tappets
	blocked filter	replace

When engine is running:

Temperature gauge high	overheating	coolant flow and/or level
Signal alarm comes 'on'	overheating	temperature gauge, coolant flow/level
		check for rise in engine room temp.
	oil pressure	level or circulation
	alternator	voltage at battery (> 13 V)

When sailing (no engine):

Decca display stops		
Radar goes to 'stand by'		
VHF crackles	low voltage	voltage test/start engine
Lights 'dim'		

When on mooring (engine off):

Fluorescent lights 'off'		
Other lights dim		
Broadcast radio whistle/ crackle	low voltage	voltage test/start engine
VHF squelch trips in